God's Secret I

Understanding Psalm 91

From Overwhelmed to Unshakeable

OTHER BOOKS BY THE AUTHOR

Alpha & Omega: The Beginning of the End - An Introduction to the End Times

Rivers of Living Water: The Holy Spirit Today

Leaving the Wilderness Behind: Lessons from the Life of Caleb

Who is Jesus of Nazareth? The Answer Will Change Your Life

At the Door: Key Nations, the Last Days, and the Coming King

Get Smart: Pearls of Wisdom from Proverbs

White Horse Coming: Seven Keys of the Book of Revelation

In the Beginning: An Introduction to the Book of Genesis

The Burdensome Stone: Jerusalem in the Last Days

The Prophet from Babylon: Understanding the Book of Daniel

The Power of Faith: Understanding the Books of Ruth and Esther

Available at tan.org.au

God's Secret Place:

Understanding Psalm 91

From Overwhelmed to Unshakeable

Kameel Majdali

Teach All Nations Inc.
Melbourne

About the author: Kameel Majdali, PhD, is the Director of Teach All Nations. An educator and global trends specialist, he teaches all over the world.

God's Secret Place: Understanding Psalm 91

Copyright © 2022 by Kameel Majdali

The author Kameel Majdali asserts his right to ownership of this book.

ISBN: 978-0-9945773-7-5

Teach All Nations Inc.
P.O. Box 493
Mount Waverley, Victoria 3149 AUSTRALIA

Requests for information contact: tan@tan.org.au

All rights reserved. No part of this book may be reproduced, stored in a retrieval system or transmitted, in any form or by any means, electronic, mechanical, photocopying or otherwise, without the prior written consent of the publisher.

Note: American and Australian words and spelling may be used interchangeably throughout this book.

Unless stated otherwise, all Scripture quotations are taken from the Authorized King James Version of the Bible (KJV). All references marked (NKJV) are from the New King James Version, copyright © 1979, 1980, 1982 by Thomas Nelson, Inc. Used by permission. All rights reserved.

Teach All Nations Inc. is a global Bible teaching ministry with a prophetic edge, based in Melbourne, Australia. For more information about the services and resources of Teach All Nations Inc., contact us at our website: tan.org.au

Our Gift to You

Thank you for purchasing *God's Secret Place*.

To show our appreciation, you are

invited to **download** a copy of our

free study guide that goes with this book.

It is suitable for personal and group study.

To obtain your copy of the study guide to *God's Secret Place*

log onto:

tan.org.au

Code: Psalm91

May you enjoy your reading of *God's Secret Place.*

CONTENTS

Dedication		09
Acknowledgements		11
Preface		13
Text of Psalm 91		15
Introduction: Why Psalm 91? Why Now?		17
Part One	Overview of Psalm 91, God, Pain and Suffering, and the Secret Place	25
Chapter One:	The God of Psalm 91	27
Chapter Two:	A Closer Look at the Secret Place and the Problem of Pain	41
Part Two	Psalm 91: Verse-by-Verse	59
Chapter Three:	Where is the Secret Place?	61
Chapter Four:	Promise of Deliverance	81
Chapter Five:	God's Truth Delivers	95
Chapter Six:	No-Fear Zone	105
Chapter Seven:	Divine Protection Reaffirmed	129
Chapter Eight:	Angels on Assignment	139

Chapter Nine:	Wild Animals Subdued	151
Chapter Ten:	Deliverance and Promotion	163
Chapter Eleven:	God's Presence, Answered Prayer and Enlargement	181
Chapter Twelve:	The Power of an Endless Life	201
Appendix One:	A Psalm 91 Prayer	223
Appendix Two:	An Appeal	225
Appendix Three:	The Promises of Trusting God	231

Dedication

To my grandchildren,
Jonas, Levi, Micah, Hadassah and Eliana.
The future belongs to you.

Acknowledgements

Appropriately, I want to thank Almighty God - to Whom we owe everything.

> *For of him, and through him, and to him, are all things: to whom be glory for ever. Amen.* — **Romans 11:36**

In addition, I want to thank some very special people.

To my book editor Heather King of Melbourne, Australia. She is immensely thorough, knowledgeable, and helpful. Though this author is not new to writing books, reading her notes has been an education. Heather's efforts and the immense amount of time invested by her are most appreciated.

Thanks are given to my faithful proofreaders Geoff and Ava Stafford of Bairnsdale, Victoria, Australia. They have always stood ready to help whenever called upon and their work is good.

Another thank you to my book publishing coach, Brett Hilker of Edmonton, Alberta, Canada. Brett works at the Self-Publishing School. He has been ultra-helpful and encouraging.

I want to also thank - and recommend - the website blueletterbible.org, which continues to be an invaluable resource for me.

Finally, but by no means least, is my wife, Leanne, whose invaluable support makes possible my ability to write and function as an author and teacher and minister-at-large. Thank you for everything.

— Kameel Majdali

Preface

Psalm 27:5: *"For in the time of trouble he shall hide me in his pavilion: in the secret of his tabernacle shall he hide me; he shall set me up upon a rock."*

Crisis: *'A time of intense difficulty, danger and trouble.'*

There is something very unwelcome when we hear the word 'crisis'; even worse are several concurrent 'crises.' Life can be challenging even in the best of times; how much more compounded the challenge becomes when difficulty knocks on the door.

Yet there is another angle from which to view crisis: danger and troubles can be the womb of opportunity. Yes, there can be positives in times of crisis. What can they be? For one, a crisis is like an alarm clock; it wakes you up from slumber and grabs your attention. During good times, it is easy to get distracted and complacent. Crisis clears up all of that, helping you to get rid of the extraneous and focus only on what matters. It can even generate revival.

Priorities come to view in crisis. If you examine how you spend your time and what is truly important, you will soon become ruthless with your prioritisation. Once seemingly important items are struck off the 'to-do list' and removed from the diary. A crisis causes you to weed things out of your schedule and life that seem necessary at the time but are superfluous. You will go from a busy, multitasking 'Martha' to a focused and devoted 'Mary' (Luke 10:38-42) when you wisely navigate through the waters of trouble. Of the two sisters, Mary made the right choice to prioritise the Lord and was highly commended by Him. Martha was patiently and lovingly encouraged to change her attitude (vv. 41-42).

Crises can be likened to growing pains. They can be unpleasant at first but when they're done, you are a bigger person. David the psalmist understood this completely. In the very first verse of the fourth psalm, he said that God enlarged him when he was in distress. There was a stretching and it was painful but once complete, the crisis gave way to promotion and a bigger field.

Most importantly, a crisis is a beckoning hand to come to God and invest in your spiritual life. Nothing is more important than this. When you make God, His kingdom, and righteousness your number one priority (Matthew 6:33), all your needs will be met, with dividends.

The third millennium began in crisis, multiple crises, and chances are that this pattern will continue. Either we can choose to worry ourselves to death, even adopt destructive behaviours. Or we can embark upon the path to divine blessing. Of course, the latter option is the only sensible one, but how do we put it into practice?

Psalm 91 is your passport, visa, and key to the victorious, internal life that rejects worry and fear, nurtures an excellent spirit and enables you to face the future with confidence. Its words are timeless and its precepts are priceless.

In *God's Secret Place: Understanding Psalm 91,* we are going to explore this wonderful psalm in depth. As we do, expect to relinquish many, even all cares, fears, apprehensions and anxieties. Welcome the peace of God as it flows into your heart and mind. Once you have been blessed, and your cup starts overflowing, be prepared to reach out and touch others who are struggling with the personal and corporate issues of the day. You will be able to impart the **Psalm 91** blessing to them too.

— Kameel Majdali 2022

Text of Psalm 91

1. He that dwelleth in the secret place of the most High shall abide under the shadow of the Almighty.
2. I will say of the LORD, He is my refuge and my fortress: my God; in him will I trust.
3. Surely he shall deliver thee from the snare of the fowler, and from the noisome pestilence.
4. He shall cover thee with his feathers, and under his wings shalt thou trust: his truth shall be thy shield and buckler.
5. Thou shalt not be afraid for the terror by night; nor for the arrow that flieth by day;
6. Nor for the pestilence that walketh in darkness; nor for the destruction that wasteth at noonday.
7. A thousand shall fall at thy side, and ten thousand at thy right hand; but it shall not come nigh thee.
8. Only with thine eyes shalt thou behold and see the reward of the wicked.
9. Because thou hast made the LORD, which is my refuge, even the most High, thy habitation;
10. There shall no evil befall thee, neither shall any plague come nigh thy dwelling.
11. For he shall give his angels charge over thee, to keep thee in all thy ways.
12. They shall bear thee up in their hands, lest thou dash thy foot against a stone.
13. Thou shalt tread upon the lion and adder: the young lion and the dragon shalt thou trample under feet.
14. Because he hath set his love upon me, therefore will I deliver him: I will set him on high, because he hath known my name.
15. He shall call upon me, and I will answer him: I will be with him in trouble; I will deliver him, and honour him.
16. With long life will I satisfy him, and shew him my salvation.

Introduction

Why Psalm 91? Why Now?

'**Psalm 91** is one of the most excellent works of this kind which has ever appeared. It is impossible to imagine anything more solid, more beautiful, more profound, or more ornamented. Could the Latin or any modern language express thoroughly all the beauties and elegances as well of the *words* as of the *sentences*, it would not be difficult to persuade the reader that we have no poem, either in *Greek* or *Latin*, comparable to this Hebrew ode' - *Simon de Muis*[i]

Whether we like it or not, as believers, we are often faced with personal challenges that can cause us intense grief, anxiety, and hardship. A loved one may be diagnosed with a terminal illness. Marriages may end or family relationships fracture. Jobs and homes might be lost. These circumstances can sometimes even cause us to question our faith and our reason to go on living.

The world is also in great turmoil. If we are in the end times - and we are - the Bible teaches that there will be a time of great turbulence. This includes *"famines, pestilences, and earthquakes"* (Matthew 24:7), along with *"wars and rumours of wars"* (v. 6). So it is not surprising that we are witnessing national and global crises of all kinds, be they of an economic, geo-political or public health nature. And we are also experiencing culture wars and increasingly intensive spiritual oppression. There is massive upheaval in the world with millions impacted by war, famine, natural disasters and persecution.

God's Secret Place

Yet our awareness of the challenges and how we handle them can make all the difference between success and failure, fruitfulness or barrenness, and personal peace as opposed to tormenting turmoil. We need a way forward.

We understand that a major reason for turbulence is that we live in a fallen world. But we are also in a time of transition from the kingdoms of this world to the kingdom of our Lord and Christ (Revelation 11:15). Transition is necessary to get to our desired haven (Psalm 107:30), but life's storms are part of the journey en route.

At the same time as we face transition and turbulence, there is the divine command: *"See that you be not troubled"* (Matthew 24:6). Sixty-three times in the Bible we are exhorted to *"fear not."* So God does not want us to worry about anything; instead, He wants us to pray about everything (Philippians 4:6).

But the question still arises: how can we reconcile these two challenges? How can we be worry-free while undergoing a time of intense end-time turbulence? Considering all the above, is there a place of refuge, a solid rock to build upon, a haven that withstands all of life's storms?

The answer to this question goes to the heart of this book. Psalm 91 teaches us that such a place does exist: God's secret place.

The Purpose and Structure of the Book

Psalm 91 is a sixteen-verse, divine masterpiece in which the Lord promises us His presence, protection, provision, and peace. It shows us the necessity and desirability of drawing near unto God at all times, not only in days of challenge. If we do this, our faith levels will rise to the occasion, and we can apprehend from God what is elusive to the unspiritual person.

Introduction: Why Psalm 91? Why Now?

This book seeks to provide you with the tools for handling the challenges and crises you can expect to face in life, without fear or loss of faith. It offers you a qualitative commentary on Psalm 91 within the Biblical context of the time, together with a detailed examination of each verse. This approach, we hope, will allow the modern reader to look behind the sometimes archaic language of the Psalm and grasp the powerful truths about God's promises that it contains.

But the book does more than this. It also seeks to give you deeper insight into God's secret place and His character, not only as revealed in Psalm 91 but also - more widely - throughout scripture. This is central to our understanding of Psalm 91 and gives us the confidence to place our complete trust in God. For this reason, Part One of the book will begin by exploring who the God of Psalm 91 is and what His Secret Place entails.

Because the promises of **Psalm 91** are so grand and sweeping, some may question whether they are too good to be true. Does God really mean that no evil shall afflict us? that no plague shall come close to our home? and that we shall enjoy total immunity from danger? Haven't righteous people suffered from all these things throughout history? What about those who are not delivered from danger or sickness? These are difficult and perplexing questions but ones to which God's Word provides answers. As a result, Part One also considers the issue of suffering and offers insights into why believers are not always exempt from hardship.

Part Two then provides a detailed examination of each of the verses in Psalm 91 and draws extensively on other parts of the Bible to supplement and illustrate the core truths of the Psalm. It uses the experience of Biblical heroes who struggled with adversity and loss to show that trust in God is never misplaced. And it also offers practical advice on how to claim the promises of Psalm 91 and apply them to your own life. In particular, it provides strategies and encouragement for those who are wrestling with pain, hardship or grief.

God's Secret Place

The Psalm's theme is clear: in a world full of change and crisis, God offers refuge, strength, and ultimate victory to those who trust and obey Him. The promises in Psalm 91 are as true today as when they were first written three thousand years ago.

As we will see, God's secret place has always been a comfort and guide, a city of refuge, and a cave of Adullam[ii] for believers throughout the centuries. Like an insurance policy, it grants us protection from the normal and unusual challenges of life. If times were normal, peaceful, and prosperous, people would feel no need to draw on this psalm's timeless counsel. Yet in light of the great shaking and aftershocks of the day, it is time to become acquainted with the psalm that can quell your fears, nurture your spirit, brighten your countenance, and plant rock-solid, divine hope into your heart.

Our goal is simple: to help inspire faith, hope, grace, and peace in the heart of the reader. This will come by understanding and applying what this great psalm says. If you build your house on the rock, then you will be able to withstand all of life's storms. You will transition from being overwhelmed to becoming unshakeable. Once that happens, you can face the present and future with confidence. Imagine the things you can do when you're not crippled by anxiety, fear, doubts, and bondage. Yet it will require a change of mind, soul, spirit and body. You will need to listen to and obey the words of God and become a Biblical practitioner by the power of the Holy Spirit. You will need to place your life solely into God's hands.

Background to Psalm 91

To better understand the truths of **Psalm 91**, it is important to set the scene with some basic background information. The psalm is at least three thousand years old. Who was the author? It was written

Introduction: Why Psalm 91? Why Now?

anonymously. While many nominate David, the sweet psalmist of Israel (2 Samuel 23:1), the Talmud makes another recommendation: Moses.[iii] He is the reputed author of the previous psalm, **Psalm 90**, and it is customary to assign the authorship of anonymous sacred writings to the last person who was named.[iv]

The notion of Mosaic authorship does have some plausibility. Israel's great prophet led his people out of the bondage yet predictability of life in Egypt. But after witnessing the ten plagues and miraculously departing from the land of the pharaohs, the Hebrews were immediately thrust into a new challenge: life in the wilderness. So Moses was well-equipped to write about the need for total dependence upon God in order to survive a harsh and dangerous environment.

Nonetheless, we cannot be absolutely sure who the author of **Psalm 91** is, nor is it essential to know. Many Old Testament books (and the Book of Hebrews) were written anonymously, and this does not detract from the authority and inspiration of the text at all. Knowing the human author of Bible books can be helpful, but it is not critical. What ultimately matters is that we know the real author - Almighty God. **Psalm 91** is His invitation to you to draw near and come into His secret place.

Is Psalm 91 Still Relevant Today?

The thing that hath been, it is that which shall be; and that which is done is that which shall be done: and there is no new thing under the sun - **Ecclesiastes 1:9**.

No doubt some will question how a psalm written in ancient times, in a different culture and geographic setting, could guide us through the maze of modern living. While circumstances and cultures change, human nature does not. The emotions, tests, actions, and reactions of the ancients are still part of what we experience today. They faced need, fear, anger, and desperation - and so do we. As **Ecclesiastes 1:9** says, the past is a prologue, and there is nothing new under the sun. History has seen it all before.

Just as human nature and our needs do not change, neither does God. He is the same yesterday, today, and forever (Hebrews 13:8). So the way God led the Hebrews long ago is how He leads us today.

After arriving in the promised land of Canaan, the Israelites faced intense challenges of wars, famine, opposition, internal strife, and betrayal. The Canaanites were not going to hand over the land on a silver platter; the Israelites had to fight for it. Indeed, God commanded them to do precisely that. But with the command came the promise of His presence (Joshua 1:1-9).

In addition, there was the prospect of divine leadership; God personally would go ahead of them and lead them to victory. And when they faced intense danger, they discovered that God was their refuge and strength (Psalm 46:1). What God did for them, He does for us today.

Our turbulent, transitional times may be difficult and draining, but there is a silver lining. Our trials give us an outstanding opportunity to recognise our need for Almighty God, not just day by day, but moment by moment. While this often grates against our carnal, independent nature, it is also a healthy place for believers to be. For when God is all we have, we quickly discover that God is all we need. Moses, David, and the other psalmists understood this principle only too well.

So we begin this study with the rock-solid conviction that **Psalm 91** is God's Word; it is true and eternal, and we cannot go wrong by taking His promises at face value. They have been tried in the fire and have come forth as gold. If things seem to be going the opposite way, we can trust the Lord to do the right thing, whether it makes sense to the natural mind or not. Let the wonderful counsel of **Proverbs 3:5-6** be our guide. If

Introduction: Why Psalm 91? Why Now?

we place our trust in God exclusively and resist the urge to rely on our instincts and experience, God promises that He will direct our footsteps on the way forward.

Who is the God of Psalm 91?

As we explore **Psalm 91**, we will learn that God doesn't just lead us to His safe space - God is Himself in that space. Therefore, it behoves us to learn more about who the God of **Psalm 91** is. It is God's character that gives us the unshakeable conviction that His promises are true.

The important thing to remember is that it is the one and only true God, maker of heaven and earth, who invites us to come and make ourselves at home 'with Him' and 'in Him.' There can, indeed, be a mystery to God's dealings, which may not be apparent to you at the time that you most need Him (Daniel 2:22; Job 12:22; Jeremiah 33:3). But Scripture emphasises that we must come to God, who is always good, and commit ourselves to Him and trust in Him at all times, even when we don't understand the situation we are in. Those wise people who do precisely this will experience protection, peace, provision, and promotion. Once we are cognisant of what God is truly offering in **Psalm 91,** we should see that it is, in truth, the proverbial offer that is 'too good to refuse.'

From here, we are ready to go deeper into Psalm 91.

---

[i] Spurgeon, C. "Psalm 91 by C. H. Spurgeon." Blue Letter Bible. Last Modified 5 Dec 2016. https://www.blueletterbible.org/Comm/spurgeon_charles/tod/ps091.cfm

God's Secret Place

[ii] The Cave of Adullam was David's special hiding place from Saul (1 Samuel 22:1-2), who actively sought to slay him. Yet Adullam was more than just a refuge: David may have written some of the psalms there and in this location he assembled his famous mighty men, around four-hundred. Not only did they help him win multiple battles on different fronts, but it was they who conquered the city of Jerusalem for David; this event alone changed history. The secret place can be a productive place.

[iii] Henry, M. "Commentary on Psalms 91 by Matthew Henry." Blue Letter Bible. Last Modified 1 Mar, 1996. https://www.blueletterbible.org/Comm/mhc/Psa/Psa_091.cfm.

[iv] Ibid.

Part One

Overview of Psalm 91, God, Pain and Suffering, and the Secret Place

Chapter One

The God of Psalm 91

Given the promises contained in Psalm 91, it is easy to focus on the benefits God can provide for those who trust in Him. Yet at the same time, we can also learn a lot about God Himself. We get a micro-theological lesson on who God is and not just what He can do for us.

This chapter is called *'The God of Psalm 91.'* Yet God is not limited to the words of one psalm. What we learn here about the Almighty is consistent with what the entire Bible reveals about Him. Let the following words and phrases take on new meanings as we explore this subject.

Who is God in Psalm 91?

He that dwelleth in the secret place of the most High shall abide under the shadow of the Almighty. 2 I will say of the LORD, He is my refuge and my fortress: my God; in him will I trust - **Psalm 91:1-2**.

By studying **Psalm 91**, we learn about God Himself. In the first two verses, we find four titles or descriptions of the Almighty. They are:

1. Most High (v. 1)
2. Almighty (v. 1)
3. LORD (v. 2)
4. My God (v. 2)

Let's look at each of these titles in turn.

God's Secret Place

Most High

The phrase 'Most High' (or עֶלְיוֹן *elyon* in Hebrew) is used fifty-three times in the Old Testament.[i] It means *'elevation, lofty, supreme, Most High, higher than any other.'*[ii] God Most High is the one and only God. There is no other. Since God is 'Most High,' He is superior to any enemy, circumstance or threat we face.

We learn more about the meaning of 'Most High' from Abraham's encounter with Melchizedek in **Genesis 14:17-20**.

Melchizidek was *"king of Salem"* (v. 18) and his name means *'king of righteousness.'*[iii] He is described as *"priest of the most high God"* (v. 19). After Abraham rescued his brother's son Lot from King Chedorlaomer, Melchizidek came out to greet him with bread and wine, saying "Blessed be Abram of the God most high, possessor of heaven and earth." On behalf of Abraham, Melchizedek also blessed *"God Most High,"* and credited Him with delivering Abraham's enemies into his hand (v. 20).

Abraham recognized Melchizidek as someone exceptional because he offered him a tithe of everything that he had (v. 20). You can read more about him in **Hebrews 7:1-22**.

Almighty God

The term 'Almighty' is used forty-eight times in the Old Testament, especially in Genesis and Job.[iv] The Hebrew word is שַׁדַּי or *Shaddai*. This means 'Almighty, all-powerful (omnipotent), who can destroy any rival or adversary who comes on the scene.'[v]

An example of *'Shaddai* Almighty God' is found in the story of Jacob in **Genesis 28:1-5**. Having stolen Isaac's blessing intended for his fraternal twin brother Esau, Jacob fled for his life to Padan Aram. Before he left the

One: The God of Psalm 91

country, his father Isaac blessed him on what became a twenty-year sojourn in a strange land with his uncle Laban.

If Jacob's Hebrew name *Yaakov* means 'heel-catcher, heal-holder, supplanter,'[vi] then our hero met his match with Laban. This wily uncle tricked Jacob into working for him for seven years in order to marry his cousin Rachel, only for him to end up instead with her sister Leah in the matrimonial tent. In addition, Laban changed Jacob's wages ten times (see Genesis 31:41-42). Yet the God of his fathers – *El Shaddai* - saw his affliction and labour, and He reimbursed and enriched him while rebuking Laban in the process. God gives overarching care to those who trust in him.

Isaac's prophetic blessing to Jacob draws on the promises that God made to Abraham when He first called on him to leave his home and travel to the land which God said He would show him (Genesis 12). In **Genesis 28**, Isaac asked God to bring those promises into fruition through his son (v. 4).

Here are the key things that Almighty God would go on to do for Jacob:

1. **Produce Fruitfulness**: Almighty God would bless, make fruitful, and multiply Jacob (v. 3). Jacob had twelve sons who became the twelve tribes of Israel;

2. **Create an Assembly of People**: *El Shaddai* would make the descendants of Abraham, Isaac, and Jacob as numerous as the stars in the sky and grains of sand on the shore;

3. **Bestow the Land of Canaan**: Jacob was given Canaan, the postage stamp of real estate promised to Abraham, together with innumerable descendants and universal blessing (v. 4). All these are tenets of the Abrahamic covenant. God said to Abraham **in Genesis**

God's Secret Place

> **22:18**: *"And in thy seed shall all the nations of the earth be blessed; because thou hast obeyed my voice."*

In fulfilling all of His promises, Almighty God displayed His faithfulness and power. But it is noteworthy that Isaac also cautioned his son, for his own protection, not to marry a Canaanite woman (v. 1). In doing so, he was remembering God's earlier warnings to the Israelites not to intermarry. God always cautions those He loves.

LORD

The term 'lord' simply means 'master.' When applied to Almighty God, it means the pinnacle of all power, majesty, might, and dominion. The Hebrew word for Lord is יְהוָה (Yehovah, Jehovah, Yahweh). It is used 6,519 times in 5,521 verses of the Old Testament.[vii] YHWH יְהוָה is known as the tetragrammaton - God's unpronounceable name.[viii]

So, yes, this word יְהוָה is God's actual name and one we cannot accurately pronounce. The reason is that we don't have the original vowels that go with the consonants. Vowels in Hebrew (nikud) are usually depicted by dots that appear above, below, or in front of consonants. Vowels were probably given to Moses, but future rabbis did not retain them for fear of violating the third commandment: *"Thou shalt not take the name of the LORD thy God in vain; for the LORD will not hold him guiltless that taketh his name in vain"* (Exodus 20:7).

But removing the vowels of the original Hebrew to prevent using God's Name in vain meant people could not use God's name at all. This presents a problem when you want to come to God's secret place or call upon His name to be saved (Romans 10:13).

But don't feel alarmed. The patriarchs Abraham, Isaac, and Jacob, who were greatly beloved of God, did not know His Name either. They only knew Him by His titles like *Jehovah-Jireh* (God my provider), *Jehovah-*

One: The God of Psalm 91

Rapha (God the healer), *Jehovah-Nissi* (God my banner) and *el Shaddai* (God Almighty).

The first time God shared His name with any mortal man was with Moses in **Exodus 6:1-4**, centuries after the patriarchs. God said that He appeared to Abraham, Isaac, and Jacob as God Almighty (*El Shaddai*); but by the Name LORD - *Yehovah* - they did not know Him.

So when you see the title LORD used in the Bible all in capital letters, that's the English version of YHWH יְהֹוָה. When read in the original Hebrew, it is pronounced *Adonai* or Lord, though there is no correlation between the letters written and the pronunciation given.

What Name Should We Use for God?

Here's the challenge then. Since God Himself is our 'secret place and safe space,' how can we reach Him if we don't have access to the one key that will open the door - His Name? In the time of need, how can we call on a God we cannot name?

Fortunately, there is a way forward with God's Name and how to pronounce it. In **Philippians 2:9-11**, we read that:

> *God also hath highly exalted him, and given him a name which is above every name: That at the name of Jesus every knee should bow ... And that every tongue should confess that Jesus Christ is Lord, to the glory of God the Father.*

So we do have a Name that we can say, which will deliver to us all the safe-space benefits that **Psalm 91** offers: refuge, peace, restoration, renewal, revival, and salvation. For as it is written in **Acts 4:12**: *"Neither is there salvation in any other: for there is none other name under heaven given among men, whereby we must be saved."*

God's Secret Place

Do you want to begin the journey into the secret place? Call on the Name of Jesus, the name above every name. Scripture says that when you call on the Name of the Lord, you will be saved (2 Samuel 22:4; Psalm 18:3; Acts 2:21; Romans 10:13).

The LORD, My LORD

While all this information is important, it is not enough. The LORD is capable of doing many, wonderful things in your life. However, something has to happen. He must go from being LORD in your life to being 'My LORD.' You must move from merely acknowledging His existence to abiding under the shadow of His wings.

How can we make this transition? When you accept the gospel of Christ and respond through repentance, faith, and obedience, then the LORD becomes your LORD because Jesus becomes your LORD. When that happens, you are on your way to claiming your spot in the secret place.

Obedience

Words alone, however, are not enough. Many people call Jesus 'LORD,' but He is not the Lord of their life. The sobering words of Jesus in **Matthew 7:21** offer a clear warning: *"Not every one that saith unto me, Lord, Lord, shall enter into the kingdom of heaven; but he that doeth the will of my Father which is in heaven."*

It is not sufficient merely to 'hear' the Word. Jesus is LORD to those who 'do' the Word - obedience is the key. On the day of judgement, some people will claim that they did many wonderful works in the Name of Jesus (v. 22) Yet He will tell them that He never knew them, and He will command them to depart because they are all workers of iniquity (v. 23). That should instil some wonderful, old-fashioned fear of the Lord.

One: The God of Psalm 91

So the key to making God your LORD is to obey the will of God the Father. After all, Jesus asks in **Luke 6:46**: *"[W]hy call ye me, Lord, Lord, and do not the things which I say?"* The question is a good one but often the answer is feeble.

Obedience is the key to developing an intimate but honouring relationship with God. King David had such a relationship with Him. In the great Messianic **Psalm 110**, David uses the phrase, *"The Lord said unto my Lord"* (v. 1). The first 'Lord' is God the Father, and He is speaking to someone different (*"my Lord"*) who was understood at the time to be the Messiah - God the Son. It was David's complete submission to God that earned him the right to call Him 'My Lord.' Can you also do this? To get the benefits of the secret place, you must go from calling God LORD, to addressing Him as 'My LORD.' Then the blessings will flow.[ix]

My God

The fourth and final name/title for God found in **Psalm 91** is simply 'my God.' The Hebrew word for God is *Elohim* אֱלֹהִים. It is used 2,606 times in 2,249 verses.[x]

God is the only God there is, and He is pleased to partner with all who will obey and put their trust in Him.

'Doubting Thomas,' after examining the resurrected Christ's nail-scarred hands and pierced side, fell on his knees and exclaimed with great astonishment: *"My Lord and my God"* (John 20:28).

Since 'Lord' means 'master,' consider what Thomas was saying. Everyone has a 'master' in their life, and it could be anything: career, money, hobby, sport, a bad habit, lust, addiction, or idolatry - the list is endless. But those who enjoy God's secret place have no other Lord but the LORD and no other God but God. Thomas covered both bases - Lord and God - and ended up being the great apostle who brought the gospel to India.

It is not sufficient to merely 'hear' the Word. Jesus is LORD to those who 'do' the Word - obedience is the key.

Can you say with confidence that 'God is my God?' Jesus said it (John 20:17); Thomas said it (John 20:28); Paul said it (Romans 1:8); and John said it (Revelation 3:12). If you are not yet in that position, then surrender to the LORD completely and trust Him perfectly. Then you will be on your way to His safe space.

The Nature of God

Finding your way to God's secret place requires a knowledge of God in general, not just in **Psalm 91**. We will look to other parts of the Bible to enlarge our understanding of the Most High God. The following points are just a few of the many aspects of God's nature. When you understand these important things, you will want to race into the secret place of the Most High, not out of necessity but desire.

The One and Only God

Thus saith the LORD the King of Israel, and his redeemer the LORD of hosts; I am the first, and I am the last; and beside me there is no God — **Isaiah 44:6**.

The Bible is emphatic that there is one, and only one, God. He is not just one among many gods or the greatest of all gods; He is singular - the one and only God. There are no other gods out there, full stop. Without beginning or end, predecessors, successors, or superiors, the God of the Bible is singular in every way.

One: The God of Psalm 91

Ye are my witnesses ... that ye may know and believe me, and understand that I am he: before me there was no God formed, neither shall there be after me — **Isaiah 43:10**.

Yes, the God who is our refuge is the only God and the only refuge. If you look for alternatives, they will either be inadequate or counterfeits. If you want the genuine safe space, come to the only God there ever was, ever is, and ever will be. Again, as God affirms earlier:

I am the first, and I am the last; and beside me there is no God.
— **Isaiah 44:6**

Make note of that phrase, *"the first and the last,"* for it applies not only to God but also to Jesus Christ - **Revelation 1:11, 17** (especially the wording found in the KJV). It affirms the singularity of God and the divinity of Christ, both of which are an important part of His power to save us.

Creator

Equally important in our understanding of the divine refuge is that God is our Creator. For eighteen centuries, the notion that God is our Creator was not seriously questioned in any credible quarters. Today, it is challenged, attacked, ridiculed, and ignored. There are reasons for this, and they have nothing to do with science. It is ultimately a moral and spiritual issue, as well as a sign of increasing last days' deception.

The implications are this: if God is our Creator, we can never be the ultimate source of power (Revelation 1:5). If God is our Creator, we will have to give an account of ourselves to Him (Romans 14:12). If God is our Creator, then we are duty bound to keep His rules or face the inevitable and dire consequences.

Consider the scriptural case for God as Creator:

- **Isaiah 40:28** refers to *"the everlasting God, the Lord, the Creator of the ends of the earth."*

- **Romans 1:25** talks of those *"[w]ho changed the truth of God into a lie, and worshipped and served the creature more than the Creator, who is blessed for ever. Amen."*

- **1 Peter 1:19** encourages us to commit our souls *"to him … as unto a faithful Creator."*

If that is not enough, the **Revelation 4:11** gives us a guided tour around the throne of God. It then concludes: *"For thou hast created all things, and for thy pleasure they are and were created."* Other scriptures confirming God as the source of all things include **Genesis 1:1; Nehemiah 9:6; Job 26:7; Psalm 102:25; Acts 14:5;** and **Hebrews 11:3.**

In light of this scriptural case, we could safely ignore the rest of the Bible. if it could be conclusively proven that God is not the Creator. God's work of salvation and redemption are closely tied to His role as Creator. If one part of His identity fails, then the rest of divine revelation collapses too. Fortunately, such proof does not exist.

Redeemer & Saviour

Behold, God is my salvation; I will trust, and not be afraid: for the LORD JEHOVAH is my strength and my song; he also is become my salvation - **Isaiah 12:2.**

The singularity of God and His paramount role in creation position Him to be our Redeemer and Saviour. As one preacher aptly put it: "Christ had to be God to save us and man to die for us."[xi] God doesn't just give salvation - He *is* our salvation. Outside of Him, there is none.

One: The God of Psalm 91

The Book of Isaiah gives us tremendous insight into the nature of God. Not only is the theme of Isaiah 'God the Saviour,' but the prophet Isaiah's name in Hebrew is *Yeshayahu* יְשַׁעְיָהוּ meaning 'the Lord has saved.' So, fittingly, in **Isaiah 43:11,** we see God proclaim: *"I, even I, am the Lord; and beside me there is no saviour."*

God offers both physical and spiritual salvation. In **Psalm 106:21,** the psalmist laments that Israel forgot *"God their saviour, which had done great things in Egypt."* But when Mary, the mother of Jesus, sang the Magnificat, she declared that her spirit rejoiced in *"God my Saviour"* (Luke 1:47). Yes, even the mother of Jesus needed a Saviour, and so do we. The birth of Jesus was announced by angels, proclaiming that in the city of David was born *"a Saviour, which is Christ the Lord"* (Luke 2:11).

As one preacher aptly put it: 'Christ had to be God to save us and man to die for us.'

There are numerous instances in the New Testament where Jesus taught that He was our Saviour. For example, the word 'saviour' is used six times in **Titus.**[xii] After Jesus sojourned with the Samaritans for a couple of days, sharing the Word, they did not need further persuasion. After hearing from Jesus first-hand, they had no difficulty in concluding that He was *"indeed the Christ, the Saviour of the world"* (John 4:42).

Consider the magnitude of it all: the one and only God - the Creator of the ends of the earth – is our Saviour and Redeemer. And He is allowing us to come to Him and find refuge from all of life's storms.

It is an offer too good to refuse. So let us now look more closely at the secret place offered by Psalm 91 and the way it can help us withstand difficult or painful situations.

.

God's Secret Place

[i] "H5945 - ʿelyôn - Strong's Hebrew Lexicon (KJV)." Blue Letter Bible. Accessed 3 Aug, 2022. https://www.blueletterbible.org/lexicon/h5945/kjv/wlc/0-1/.

[ii] Ibid.

[iii] Hebrews 7:2.

[iv] "H7706 - šaday - Strong's Hebrew Lexicon (kjv)." Blue Letter Bible. Accessed 3 Aug, 2022. https://www.blueletterbible.org/lexicon/h7706/kjv/wlc/0-1/.

[v] Ibid.

[vi] "H3290 - yaʿăqōḇ - Strong's Hebrew Lexicon (kjv)." Blue Letter Bible. Accessed 19 Aug, 2022. https://www.blueletterbible.org/lexicon/h3290/kjv/wlc/0-1/.

[vii] "H3068 - Yĕhovah - Strong's Hebrew Lexicon (KJV)." Blue Letter Bible. Accessed 20 Apr, 2020. https://www.blueletterbible.org//lang/lexicon/lexicon.cfm?Strongs=H3068&t=KJV.

[viii] https://www.christianity.com/wiki/christian-terms/what-is-the-tetragrammaton-meaning-and-usage.html.

[ix] **Point of interest - Judah & Jehovah**: The Name of God - the tetragrammaton - is found within the name of Judah. There is only one letter difference, the daleth in Judah (ד). It is the head tribe (Genesis 49:10) and the one from which Christ came. Judah is where we get the name 'Jew' or 'Jewish.'

Jehovah = יְהֹוָה

Judah = יְהוּדָה

A Messianic scholar explains the irrational, rampant anti-Semitism throughout history. God's Name is found in Judah's, therefore, the reason the world hates the Jewish people (Judah) is that the world hates God (John 15:18-25). Dov Chaikin, *The Biblical Origins of Anti-Semitism: Israel Today*, 1 June 2016, https://www.israeltoday.co.il/read/the-biblical-origins-of-anti-semitism/.

One: The God of Psalm 91

[x] "H430 - 'elohiym - Strong's Hebrew Lexicon (KJV)." Blue Letter Bible. Accessed 20 Apr, 2020. https://www.blueletterbible.org//lang/lexicon/lexicon.cfm?Strongs=H430&t=KJV.

[xi] Bob Gass, author of the daily devotional *The Word for Today.*

[xii] Titus 1:3; 1:4; 2:10,13; 3:4,6.

Chapter Two

A Closer Look at the Secret Place and the Problem of Pain

The promise of God to provide a secret place in **Psalm 91** is not an aberration. It is not an exception to the rule or a one-off promise. It is part of a greater story of the Good Shepherd who takes care of His sheep. He leads, feeds, guides, provides, protects, and defends His flock, as **Psalm 23** so faithfully attests. **Psalm 91** is God's Word for saints in trouble. But Psalm 91 does not promise to eliminate or negate hard times. While we are in this corrupt world, suffering will happen. But we know that God can provide a secret place in times of trouble. He can keep us from trouble altogether. Or He will be present with us in trouble.

The Bible records numerous situations where God provided a safe place to his servants in times of difficulty or privation. These examples span thousands of years and illustrate that those who placed their trust in God reaped the benefits. But we will also see that God's provision is not just historic. He has also made future provisions for believers when they encounter difficulties during the period which marks the beginning of End Times. So let us take a walk through Scripture and understand that because God cares, God protects. He may allow suffering, but He never leaves us nor forsakes us (Hebrews 13:5). Consider the following stories.

Noah's Ark

But Noah found grace in the eyes of the LORD - **Genesis 6:8**.

God's Secret Place

Most people would be familiar with the story of Noah's Ark. After witnessing unspeakable sin, depravity, and debauchery, God decided enough was enough: He wiped the slate clean by bringing a universal flood to cleanse the earth. This was His 'just side,' but God was equally merciful. He demonstrated this by directing Noah to build an ark. It was a way of escape from the ultimate of storms.

While some sceptics dismiss the notion of a universal flood, an ark, or both, it is good to be reminded that Jesus Christ believed and promoted this narrative. He identified the period before His second coming as the 'days of Noah' (Matthew 24:37-38; Luke 17:26-27). For Him, it was not some sort of folklore or mythology but a historical fact. The Lord has absolute credibility because He is the Son of God and He spoke only what the Father directed Him to say (John 12:49).

Isaac's Rehoboth

"And he moved from there and dug another well; and they did no quarrel over it. So he called its name Rehoboth, because he said, For now the LORD has made room for us, and we shall be fruitful in the land" - **Genesis 26:22** (NKJV).

God chose the Jewish people to be a light to the nations. The story began when He directed the patriarch Abraham to leave his own home in Ur of the Chaldees (Genesis 11:31) and go to the country that God would show him (Genesis 12:1). Subsequently, in obedience to God's command, Abraham's son Isaac also dwelt in Canaan, the land promised to his father. This was not easy because the land was arid; and at that time, it was afflicted with drought and famine. The key was that God promised to be with Isaac, **provided** he obeyed God's command to stay where He had sent him. Isaac did remain and so he prospered, despite the dire circumstances.

Two: A Closer Look at the Secret Place

Isaac's obedience to God did not guarantee a trouble-free existence. Indeed, his prosperity and success caused great envy amongst, and harassment by, the local Philistines, which led Isaac to a special place called 'Rehoboth.' Rehoboth (meaning 'room') was a 'Philistine-free zone' that provided fruitfulness, water in a dry land, and no strife at all. Most of all, it was a divine secret place. It is time to include Rehoboth in your faith itinerary.[i]

Jacob's Peniel

And Jacob called the name of the place Peniel: for I have seen God face to face, and my life is preserved - **Genesis 32:30**.

Isaac's son Jacob was also singled out by God to play a special role in His plans for Israel and was blessed abundantly by Him. Peniel - the place where Jacob encountered God face to face - goes hand-in-hand with God's sanctuary in **Psalm 91**. As is often the case, trial and trouble preceded Jacob's arrival at Peniel. Not only was he tricked by his uncle Laban into marrying his daughter Leah when his heart lay with her sister Rachel. But later, when he sought to return to Canaan in secret with his family and livestock, his uncle also followed in hot pursuit. Jacob also experienced one of the most stressful moments of his life when he faced a potential physical conflict with his brother Esau, whose birthright he had stolen. One false move and he could lose everything he held dear including his life. Much was at stake.

Paradoxically, it was domesticated Jacob, not his more athletic twin brother Esau, who had a wrestling match with the Angel of God. The heavenly being gave him a new name 'Israel' - Prince of God and/or He who strives (Genesis 32:28). So his secret place was called 'Peniel' or 'face of God.' Normally, at that time, it was believed that if you saw God, you would die. In **Exodus 33:20**, for example, God told Moses: *"Thou canst not see my face: for there shall no man see me, and live."* Yet not only did Jacob survive - he thrived - and got a new name and nature as a bonus.

God's Secret Place

Psalm 91 also promises that we will be able to get very close to the face of God and yet live.

Joseph's Storehouse

Let Pharaoh do this, and let him appoint officers over the land, and take up the fifth part of the land of Egypt in the seven plenteous years. 35 And let them gather all the food of those good years that come, and lay up corn under the hand of Pharaoh, and let them keep food in the cities. 36 And that food shall be for store to the land against the seven years of famine, which shall be in the land of Egypt; that the land perish not through the famine - **Genesis 41:34-36.**

Joseph, the youngest son of Jacob/Israel, had youthful dreams of being a premier leader. His dream eventually came to pass but only via the pathway of servanthood and adversity. His jealous older brothers sold him into slavery, and he was imprisoned in Egypt. But with God's hand upon his life, he rose to a position of influence in the Pharoah's household and eventually ensured the survival of the people who would go on to form the great nation of Israel. In any case, the Lord clearly showed him that there would be seven years of plentiful harvest in Egypt followed by seven years of famine. To survive this catastrophe required prudence and planning.

The secret place here was Joseph's storehouse in Egypt, which held the excess grain for the time of scarcity. God's purpose of leadership for Joseph wasn't to raise him up for his own sake; it was to preserve life during famine and guarantee the fulfilment of God's promises to Abraham (Genesis 45:5; Genesis 17:6). Jacob's entire family moved to Egypt at Joseph's behest and it became the ideal place for the Hebrews to acquire the skills and resilience essential for nationhood and to learn to trust God.

Two: A Closer Look at the Secret Place

The Torah's 'Cities of Refuge'[ii]

> *Speak to the children of Israel, and say to them: 'When you cross the Jordan into the land of Canaan, 11 then you shall appoint cities to be cities of refuge for you, that the manslayer who kills any person accidentally may flee there.'*
> - **Numbers 35:10-11** (NKJV).

The cities of refuge could possibly be regarded as the most 'official' of all of God's safe spaces. After leading the Hebrews out of Egypt to the borders of Canaan, Moses, at God's behest, directed Israel to set up six cities of refuge, three west of the Jordan River and three to the east.[iii] The purpose was to protect someone who committed involuntary manslaughter (such protection was not given to those who committed premeditated murder). Those seeking to escape retribution could flee to one of these cities to protect themselves from the avenger of blood. Once the high priest died, then the refugee was free to go home.

The ancient Middle East had a strong culture of honour and vengeance. If one of their own was killed, even accidentally, family members may have felt compelled to avenge the death. The city of refuge reflects the mercy and protection of God and serves as a template for 'God's Secret Place.'

Ruth and The Wings of the Lord

> *The LORD recompense thy work, and a full reward be given thee of the LORD God of Israel, under whose wings thou art come to trust* - **Ruth 2:12**.

The Book of Ruth tells of a Moabite woman who chose to remain with her Jewish mother-in-law Naomi after the deaths of her father-in-law and husband. Ruth not only adopted Naomi's country but also Naomi's God - the God of Israel. Though Moab is close to Judah geographically, Ruth's spiritual journey was enormous.

God's Secret Place

Loyal, hard-working and devoted, Ruth found favour with an affluent and righteous Jewish man, Boaz, who was distantly related to her father-in-law. They married, had a son named Obed, and thus preserved the Messianic lineage via Judah (Genesis 49:10). Ruth is named as one of the ancestors of Christ in **Matthew 1:5**.

The Book of Ruth is more than just a beautiful tale of love. Ruth went from utter destitution and hopelessness to blessing and triumph. How did this happen? Her story is a manifesto of redemption. All this was made possible because Ruth transferred her allegiance and trust from the false gods of the Moabites,[iv] her biological people, to the God of Israel, her adopted people. She entrusted herself 'under the wings of the Lord.' This is an echo of **Psalm 91**.

The Psalmist's Hiding Place

Thou art my hiding place; thou shalt preserve me from trouble; thou shalt compass me about with songs of deliverance. Selah - **Psalm 32:7**.[v]

We also find God described as a 'hiding place.' In addition, **Psalm 46:1** calls God *"our refuge and strength."* There are so many examples of God's providing sanctuary to His people, not only in the Scriptures but also in modern times. David - the anointed King, psalmist, and the beloved of the Lord - experienced much more trial and heartache than most Godly people will ever face. God delivered him from his enemies on numerous occasions. Yet David also learned an invaluable lesson in them all: the distress that God allowed in his life was for growth and enlargement (see Psalm 4:1; 18:18-19; 118:5).

More recently, this aspect of God's secret place was immortalised in the book and movie titled *'The Hiding Place,'* featuring the victorious life story of evangelist Corrie ten Boom (1892-1983). Ten Boom was an unmarried Dutch woman who lived with her sister and father in Holland. They hid Jewish people from the Nazis during World War II.

Two: A Closer Look at the Secret Place

Eventually, she and her sister Betsy were betrayed, arrested, and sent by the Nazis to the infamous women's Ravensbruck concentration camp, north of Berlin. During their confinement, they had Bible studies and led other women prisoners to the Lord. Though Betsy died at the camp, by a miracle - a clerical error - Corrie escaped the gas chamber and spent the rest of her life as an evangelist, preaching victory in Jesus and practising forgiveness of her captors.

God's Name

Proverbs 18:10 speaks of God's Name as a *"high tower"* into which the righteous run and are safe. As we see here, the Name of the Lord gives access to safety as well as salvation. Since we do not yet see God, His Name becomes the key that unlocks the door to all of heaven's benefits, including divine protection and salvation. As **Proverbs 30:5** says: *"Every word of God is pure: he is a shield unto them that put their trust in him."* The Word is pure, it inspires faith, and once exercised, you will enjoy the Lord as a shield. **Psalm 46:1** calls God our refuge and strength.

Ephesians 6 speaks about spiritual warfare and the need for us to put on the whole armour of God in order to withstand the stratagems of the enemy (vv. 14-17).[vi] The details are striking. But even though there is no direct mention of God's Name, no aspect of God's armour can be used without it. Nor is prayer in the Spirit (v. 18) possible. Trying to follow God without knowing His Name is like trying to start an automobile without the key.

Of course, **Psalm 91** has several wonderful descriptions of the safe space, which we will explore at length.

Nahum and the Divine Stronghold

The LORD is good, a stronghold in the day of trouble; and he knoweth them that trust in him - **Nahum 1:7**.

God's Secret Place

The prophet Nahum warned the Assyrian people that He was going to bring about the destruction of their capital Nineveh as judgment for their wicked ways. His prophecy offered both caution and encouragement. As Nineveh learned from the prophecy of Nahum,[vii] the last days would be a time of unprecedented trouble. In the case of Israel, there was hope that God would hold its long-term oppressor to account. Similarly, there is hope for believers. God is good and a stronghold in the day of trouble. And God, like the good shepherd, knows all the people who trust in Him. For them, the Almighty promises refuge during their hard times.

Zephaniah's Hidden Place

Seek ye the LORD, all ye meek of the earth, which have wrought his judgment; seek righteousness, seek meekness: it may be ye shall be hid in the day of the LORD's anger - **Zephaniah 2:3**.

The prophet Zephaniah prophesied judgment upon Assyria, Israel, and the nations of the world. He gives a detailed and very bleak picture of the great and terrible 'day of the Lord' - the day of our accountability to God and justice for sin against the Lord (see Zephaniah 1:14-18). But yet again, there is hope for the meek. They are invited to seek humility and righteousness. Their reward is that *"it may be that [they] will be hidden in the day of the LORD's anger"* (Zephaniah 2:3, NKJV).

New Testament Examples

Promises of refuge are not limited to the Old Testament. One of the earliest events in the New Testament was the God-ordained flight to Egypt from 'the land of Israel'[viii] by the holy family (Joseph, Mary and the young Jesus). Warned of impending danger by God's angel, they fled out of the country to escape Herod the Great's evil plan to destroy their son. Why the need to flee? It was because Jesus was born 'king of the Jews,' whereas Herod was only the Roman-appointed king. The paranoid potentate tolerated no rivals (Matthew 2:13-23).

Two: A Closer Look at the Secret Place

Then there's Jesus' promise to believers in **Luke 21:18** that they will receive supernatural protection in the 'end times.' After giving them portents of these end times and warning them that they would be hated for His name's sake (v. v9-17), Jesus then reassured them that *"not an hair of [thei]r head [would] perish."*

The Lord goes on to say in **Luke 21:36**:

Watch ye therefore, and pray always, that ye may be accounted worthy to escape all these things that shall come to pass, and to stand before the Son of man.

Escape from what things? Jesus was referring to the calamitous events of the tribulation period, which will precede the second coming of Jesus to earth and the establishment of His Kingdom here. Parallel chapters to **Luke 21** include **Matthew 24** and **Mark 13**. All three gospels are unanimous about the perilous nature of these last days. Just as Zephaniah did, Christ is offering a prophetic early-warning service to His people. He highlights the challenges while giving a way of escape to those who heed the counsel of the above verse.

Through His beloved Apostle John in the **Book of Revelation**, which speaks about end-time events and God's coming kingdom, Jesus gave a similar promise of protection from the hour of tribulation to the Philadelphian church – the sixth of the seven churches addressed in Revelation 2-3. Philadelphia was a city in what is now modern-day Turkey. The Lord acknowledged the Philadelphian believers' faithfulness, despite persecution; and He promised to preserve them safely from the trials which He had previously indicated will come upon the earth in end times. In **Revelation 3:10**, He told them:

Because thou hast kept the word of my patience, I also will keep thee from the hour of temptation, which shall come upon all the world, to try them that dwell upon the earth.

This promise of protection is a promise worth claiming.

The Question of Suffering

So far we have been looking at the refuge or safe place that God offers us. But the examples we have seen show that suffering is part of the human condition, even for a Psalm 91 believer.

For many, there is an obvious and victorious escape. But what about the faithful ones who suffer and do not escape? In **Hebrews 11:35**, for example, we are told that *"[w]omen received their dead raised to life again: and others were tortured, not accepting deliverance; that they might obtain a better resurrection."* In this verse, we see that some people, by faith, received their dead brought back to life again. But there are others, also in faith, who were tortured, possibly to the point of death.

The subsequent verses in **Hebrews 11:36-38** go on to speak of people of faith who experienced mocking, flogging, chains, imprisonment, stoning, and temptation. Some even were sawn in two or killed by the sword. There are further examples of those who, whilst not killed, led lives of destitution and faced mistreatment and rejection. They wandered through deserts, mountains, dens and caves. Despite all these afflictions, there is no hint in **Hebrews 11** that those who suffered had less faith or were less worthy in God's eyes than those who visibly triumphed.

What are we to make of this? The question of why believers experience pain and suffering is not an easy one, but there are solid, sound, Biblical answers. Having a 'theology of suffering' will help us to make sense of painful and challenging situations and give us the means to handle them. God is more than ready to help us through pain, hardship, and grief, but we must come to Him on His terms, in His timing, and on His territory.

Two: A Closer Look at the Secret Place

Why Suffering? Our Fallen World

First of all, let us remember the Biblical view that 'God is righteous but the world is corrupt.' The entire consensus of Scripture is that God is good; He cannot be otherwise. God is good all of the time. What He created was declared 'good,' and this is no wonder because goodness is His very nature.

Yet while God is good all of the time, the world is bad. When we say 'world,' we don't mean planet earth; it is the 'world system and order' that we have in mind. Indeed, we learn that while God created the world 'good,' it became 'bad' through the sin and fall of Adam in **Genesis 3**. It is, therefore, vital that you see the spiritual nature of your suffering and any obstacles or opposition that you may be facing. Your real enemy is not the one you can see. He is the one you cannot see. He has a name: Satan. He is the adversary of all the people of God, and He has dutiful minions called demons. As Paul writes in **Ephesians 6:12**, *"we wrestle not against flesh and blood, but against principalities, against powers, against the rulers of the darkness of this world, against spiritual wickedness in high places."*

In a fallen world, bad things happen to good people, and good things happen to bad people. As Jesus Himself observed, it rains on the just and the unjust (Matthew 5:45); and the tares (a poisonous species of rye-grass) and weeds grow side-by-side with the wheat (Matthew 13:24-30).

God's Solution

People often blame God for the challenging circumstances in their lives, yet it is unreasonable to do so. It wasn't God's fault that Adam sinned - it was Adam's. Yet despite this, people often still ask why God doesn't do something to rectify this situation. The answer is that He did do something. He sent His Son to this planet to be the 'last Adam' (1 Corinthians 15:45) in order to help turn many to righteousness. Just as the 'first Adam' sinned and this brought forth death, the 'last Adam' through righteousness is the conduit for eternal life.

As we will see in the final chapter, God also promises the coming of His kingdom and the heavenly Jerusalem on earth (Revelation 21:2,10), a place where righteousness, peace, and joy find a permanent home. But until this occurs, there will always be sin and death in our world. In the meantime, believers still have access to God, who tells us that He causes all things to work together for our good (Romans 8:28), even if the actual circumstances are bad. This is what gives us hope; and it provides the key to enduring, even if we don't fully understand why our lives can be so challenging at times.

Suffering in Context

When we suffer, it is tempting to think we are the only ones and that our circumstances are worse than everyone else's. This is not so. The Apostle Peter warned that we should not be surprised by hard times, noting that these are sent to test us: *"Beloved, think it not strange concerning the fiery trial which is to try you, as though some strange thing happened unto you"* (1 Peter 4:12).

Suffering and strength can also go hand in hand since God will not allow us to suffer beyond what we can endure (1 Corinthians 10:13). He always provides a way to cope with the trial if we trust Him.

In suffering, it also helps to look unto Jesus, the author and finisher of our faith (Hebrews 12:2). Consider what He suffered on our behalf: much rejection from family, His Nazareth neighbours, His disciples (John 6:66), the religious establishment, and the Roman ruling elite. He suffered misunderstanding, grotesque mob justice, mocking, and murderous hatred.

Two: A Closer Look at the Secret Place

Hebrews 12:2 tells us that because of the joy set before Him, Jesus despised the shame and endured the cross. He dragged it through the streets of Jerusalem until Simon of Cyrene carried it on his behalf. Nails were pounded into his hands, a spear thrust into his side, and He suffered excruciating pain in a humiliating state of near-nakedness. There were also cruel taunts from enemies while he was suffering. After six hours of crucifixion, He died and was buried in a borrowed tomb. All of this Jesus suffered as the price for our redemption (1 Peter 2:24).

Remembering this can help us not to become discouraged in our souls (Hebrews 12:3).

Faith and Endurance Lessons

Trials provide invaluable lessons of faith. Naturally, we would all prefer God to keep us from trouble completely, but in a fallen world, that is not always possible. Sometimes, God deliberately allows hardship or pain to come our way to strengthen our reliance upon Him. God's presence and delivering power are often best experienced in times of trouble (Psalm 46). Suffering provides an incentive to press into His presence, and it is imperative that we do so. The doorway to the throne of grace is ever open to us (Hebrews 4:16), and trouble propels us there. Can you find any better place to be than in the secret place and shadow of the Almighty?

Then there are periods when God appears to be silent, and you simply don't know what is going on. It is in times like these that your faith and trust levels will be manifest; and if you trust and obey, you will see the glory of God. As you will see, this is what Psalm 91 promises us.

Peter's first epistle is dedicated to encouraging the suffering church and promotes the spiritual state or attitude of 'patient endurance.' Indeed, he encourages us to *"rejoice, inasmuch as ye are partakers of Christ's sufferings; that, when his glory shall be revealed, ye may be glad also with exceeding joy"* (1

God's Secret Place

Peter 4:12). Suffering strengthens the inner person and makes us stronger. Those who have suffered greatly, but not as a result of personal sin, are strong people who are being stretched by the Almighty.

Discipline as a Child of God

One of the great truths of Scripture is that when we come to God through the gospel of Christ, we become His children. This means we are his heirs, which also makes us joint heirs with Christ (Romans 8:17). Do these promises sound glorious? They are; but they also mean that just as Christ suffered, we can expect to suffer with Him. My pastor, who was no stranger to God's presence, once said that if you seek His glory, you are praying in the troubles. The suffering is the down payment to glory, like labour pains before childbirth.

Discipline is proof we are the children of God. Our suffering can often be the 'chastening of the Lord.' **Proverbs 3:11-12** speak about this explicitly. Don't despise God's chastening or be weary when He corrects you. It is a sign of God's love towards the child in whom He delights. A parallel passage found in **Hebrews 12:5-6** tells us that God's chastening means God's love. He scourges every child whom He receives. The redemptive purpose of divine chastening is mentioned in **1 Corinthians 11:32**, where we are told that God disciplines us so that we are not condemned along with the world. Without the sting of divine discipline, a person faces an eternity of regret (1 Peter 4:17).

The Suffering of the Lord

As always, we are in good company with the Saviour Himself. The Triune God made His first-ever, public appearance at the baptism of Jesus in the Jordan River. God the Son was in the water; God the Holy Spirit descended from heaven like a dove and landed on Him, and God the Father was the voice that spoke from heaven. What did He say? *"This is my beloved Son, in whom I am well pleased"* (Matthew 3:17).

Two: A Closer Look at the Secret Place

In the parallel passage found in Mark's gospel, note what happened right after this public commendation. Immediately, the Spirit of God drove Jesus into the wilderness (Mark 1:12). The Son of God - who well pleased the Father and was publicly crowned by the Holy Spirit - was now led by the Spirit into the wildness to be tempted of the devil.

It would be a tough forty days, especially since the Lord was fasting. At no point did He chafe at His plight. Instead, He exercised empowered, earth-inheriting meekness that led Him into even greater power and authority before He commenced His earthly ministry.

If God did that to His beloved Son, don't be surprised that He does it to you too. Discipline is not a mark of rejection, contempt, or indifference. On the contrary, it is a sign that we belong to Him. So in Romans 8:14-17, we learn that our sonship (women included) is manifested when we are led by the Holy Spirit, who bears witness that we are God's children. The Spirit of adoption allows us to call God 'Abba' – the Hebrew word for 'Father.' As children and joint-heirs of Christ, we may expect at times to suffer as He did so that, eventually, we can all receive glory together.

Sometimes our suffering may seem unbearable. It can even bring us to our knees. But it is in these moments that it is important always to remember that God's promises to be with us at all times are very real.

God's Presence

Jesus promised that He would always be with us *"even unto the end of the world"* (Matthew 28:20), and He reassured us that He would *"never leave [us], nor forsake [us]"* (Hebrews 13:5). This is so even if we don't 'feel' like God is with us. God's Word is true, and everything else that contradicts it is not the truth. He has promised to be with us, and Numbers 23:19 tells us that *"God is not a man that He should lie."* We know with absolute certainty that if God has said so, then He shall do it. And if He has spoken, then He shall make it good (Numbers 23:19).

So if the purpose of trouble and trials is to propel us into God's presence - which includes a greater spiritual experience, maturity, and opportunity for miracles - what can we expect? We will see the salvation of the Lord. We just need to keep standing on and proclaiming God's Word. In so doing, we can be confident that our faith will be uplifted and released, and that mountains will start moving out of the way.

With all of this in mind, let us turn now to an in-depth examination of Psalm 91 - God's lifeline for believers in trouble.

---

[i] As you read the account of Isaac in Genesis 26, note that it is a textbook case of a person exercising Biblical meekness who inherits the earth (Psalm 37:11; Matthew 5:5).

[ii] *Torah* (Greek *Pentateuch*) are the first five books of the Bible, known as the 'Five Books of Moses:' Genesis, Exodus, Leviticus, Numbers, and Deuteronomy. The last four contain what became known as the 'Law of Moses.'

[iii] Here is a list of the cities of refuge. West of the Jordan River: (1) Kadesh, in Naphtali; (2) Shechem, in Mount Ephraim; (3) Hebron, in Judah. 2. East of the Jordan River: (1) Golan, in Bashan; (2) Ramoth-Gilead, in Gad; and (3) Bezer, in Reuben.

[iv] Chemosh, meaning 'destroyer,' was the Moabite fish god (Numbers 21:29; Jeremiah 48:7, 13, 46). His worship was officially launched in Israel by Solomon (1 Kings 11:7) but ceased under Josiah (2 Kings 23:1, 13).

[v] See also **Psalm 119:114:** *"Thou art my hiding place and my shield: I hope in thy word."*

[vi] This is covered again in Chapter Ten: Deliverance and Promotion and in the section entitled *Spiritual Warfare & Promotion*.

Two: A Closer Look at the Secret Place

[vii] **Note**: Nineveh was spared because it responded positively to the preaching of Jonah (760 BC); a century later the prophet Nahum came, prophesied against Nineveh (around 663 BC), and there was no escape. The great city succumbed in 612 BC due to an invasion by the Medes and Babylonians.

[viii] Matthew's gospel uses the phrase twice (2:20,21).

Part Two

Psalm 91: Verse-by-Verse

CHAPTER THREE

Where is the Secret Place?

He that dwelleth in the secret place of the most High shall abide under the shadow of the Almighty. 2 I will say of the LORD, He is my refuge and my fortress: my God; in him will I trust — **Psalm 91:1-2**.

In this chapter, we begin with a brief overview of the content and structure of Psalm 91. We then embark upon a detailed examination of each verse of this extraordinary psalm. You will find the full text of Psalm 91 set out at the front of this book.

Overview and Outline of Psalm 91

The Psalm begins by getting straight to the point. Those who dwell in the secret place of the most High will live under His shadow. God becomes a refuge, fortress, and our God; we belong to Him and He to us. Once this happens, His delivering power is activated to deal with a variety of dangers: man-made dangers, plagues, diseases, nightly terrors, war by day and/or midday destruction. While the believer may witness some frightful scenes, even up-close, nothing will touch them.

Making God our refuge and fortress is our bulwark against plagues and all kinds of evil. God will do whatever it takes to preserve us, even if it means dispatching angels on our behalf. Wild animals, those that normally strike fear in the heart of people, will be under our feet.

In the final three verses, God Himself speaks to us. The person who loves God will be delivered, promoted, and receive answered prayer from the Almighty. Though we may still face trouble, God promises to be present

God's Secret Place

with us **in** the trouble before delivering us (after all, you have to be 'in' trouble before God can get you 'out'). The faithful one will be crowned with honour, longevity, and great salvation. This is the splendour of **Psalm 91**.

The following brief outline of the structure of the Psalm will provide a useful overview or 'roadmap' for you. Many psalms have an official title, but Psalm 91 does not.

I. Introduction (vv.1-2)

    A. Dwelling in the secret place of the Most High (v. 1)
    B. Declaration of refuge (v. 2)

II. The Promise (vv. 3-6)

    A. God will surely deliver you from (v. 3)

        1. The snare of the fowler
        2. The perilous pestilence

    B. Promised method of deliverance (v. 4)

        1. Covered with feathers
        2. Trusting Him under His wings

    C. Freedom from fear (vv. 5-6)

        1. From the terror by night (v. 5)
        2. From the arrow that flies by day
        3. From the pestilence that walks in darkness (v. 6)
        4. From the destruction that lays waste at midday

Three: Where is the Secret Place?

    D. Visible Deliverance (vv. 7-8)

        1. A thousand will fall at the side (v. 7)
        2. Ten thousand shall fall at your right hand yet ...
        3. It will not come to you
        4. You will see the destruction but you will be untouched (v. 8)

    E. A grand promise (vv. 9-10)

        1. Because you have made God your refuge (v. 9)
        2. No evil will befall you (v. 10)
        3. No plague will come near your dwelling

    F. Mechanics of deliverance - the angels (vv. 11-12)

        1. God will commission His angels to keep you at all times (v. 11)
        2. They will hold you up lest you dash your foot (v. 12)

    G. Daring and Empowered - You will tread on (v. 13)

        1. The lion
        2. The adder
        3. The young lion
        4. The dragon - under your feet

III. God Speaking (vv. 14-16)

        1. Those who love God will be delivered (v. 14)
        2. Those who know His Name will be promoted
        3. Those who pray to God will receive answers (v. 15)
        4. God will be present with them in times of trouble
        5. They will be delivered and honoured.
        6. They will enjoy long life (v. 16)
        7. They will see the salvation of the Lord

God's Secret Place

Where Is the Secret Place?

The first two verses of Psalm 91 affirm that there is no better place to go than God's secret place in times of trouble. There you will find stability when there is shaking, a refuge in the face of revolt, and tranquillity where there is turmoil. Not only does Scripture describe it - it beckons you to come.

Years ago, my mother was visiting her family in Los Angeles. It was 6:00 am. Suddenly, her bedroom began to shake, the overhead light swung like a pendulum, and then her bed began to move around the room. Most ominous of all, the earth began to growl beneath her.

All of this lasted a long terrifying sixty seconds. Yet that was not all. Throughout that day, the process began all over again, and the serenity was broken. Of course, many of you will know what this was: a Californian earthquake and its aftershocks.

In times like these, where can you go for refuge? We need to learn that the secret place we seek is not *geographical* but *spiritual*. That's not to say that the experience will neither be physical nor practical - it can be. But the Word of God is our guide, particularly **Psalm 91**.

Yet we should *not* wait until an emergency erupts to look for the secret place. Now is the time to identify and locate it. It will take us from sinking sands to solid rock and from panic to peace.

Pathway to Peace (v. 1)

Psalm 91 wastes no time with introductions. The opening words tell us that when we want to find and live in that special interior place of God, we come not to the place only but to God Himself. As the opening verse avers, the benefits come to those who dwell *"in the secret place of the most High"* (Psalm 91:1).

Three: Where is the Secret Place?

Key Words: Dwell and Abide (v. 1)

If we are going to understand what is offered in **Psalm 91,** we will need to know the meaning of keywords. Personal experience shows that having insight into just one key Bible word can be life-changing. Two key words in verse 1 are 'dwell' and 'abide.' They overlap in meaning.

Dwell

'Dwell,' which in Biblical Hebrew is *yashab* יָשַׁב, is used 1,088 times in the Hebrew Bible and means: 'dwell (437 times); 'inhabitant' (221 times), 'sit' (172 times), 'abide' (70 times), and 'inhabit' (39 times), among other meanings. In short, *yashab* - 'dwell' - means 'to sit down, stay, and dwell in your (new, permanent, and safe) abode.'[i]

To dwell involves more than a visit, having a meal, or even participating in a grand banquet. To dwell means to 'make yourself at home.' There is plenty of room for everyone in the secret place of the Most High, yet unfortunately, only the minority will find it.

Abide

'Abide' comes from the Hebrew *luwn* לוּן, which is used eighty-seven times in the Hebrew Bible. It means to 'lodge, pass the night, abide, remain (fig.), cause to rest or lodge.'[ii] **Psalm 91** calls us to "*abide under the shadow of the Almighty.*" This abiding implies that we have access and proximity to God and that, in effect, we live with Him. We are part of His household and belong there permanently. If you were offered quality, permanent quarters in the royal palace, would you take it? The 'secret place of the Most High' is precisely that and more since it is offered by the King of kings and Lord of lords.

Using an all-too-familiar analogy, there are some people who come and pay a brief visit to a country. They are on a 'tourist visa.' Next up the ladder are those who are 'temporary residents.' They can stay longer than tourists can, but they are not citizens and do not have citizen rights. Their legal status is in no way secure or permanent. Then there are permanent residents: they have the right to live permanently in the country, but they don't have all of a citizen's rights and, in theory, rules can change. The only safe category is 'citizenship,' with the passport of that nation. Not only can you live in the country all your days and enjoy the benefits, but you are entitled to protection locally and when you travel overseas. You are free to go in and out. Yet at the same time, you are required to assume the responsibilities of a citizen.

Is your walk with the Lord as a tourist, temporary resident, permanent resident, or citizen of the everlasting kingdom? Citizens in God's secret place are subjects of the King and know how to 'abide' in the land.

But it is important to remember that this is a 'secret place.' Even though its existence is revealed in the Word, it is hidden from many, and its existence is not apparent. It can even be a secret for true believers.

How do We Abide in God?

Since it is *God's* secret place, we look to *God* to take us there. We won't be able to find it on our own, because it is both secret and spiritual. But do not worry - the good shepherd knows how to find and guide His sheep into their desired haven.

Jesus Christ had some important words to say about 'abiding' or 'dwelling' in Him. They are found in **John 15:1-11.** Using the metaphor of the grapevine, the Lord urged His disciples:

> *Abide in me and I in you ... As the branch cannot bear fruit of itself, except I abide in the vine, no more can ye, except ye abide in me ... I am the vine, ye are the branches: He that abideth in me, and I in him, the same bringeth forth much fruit: for without me ye can do nothing* (John 15:4-5)**.**

Three: Where is the Secret Place?

This simple passage is the key to entry into God's secret place. To arrive at and remain there, we have to lay down our tourist mindset and take up the mantle of a citizen. This requires new thinking, new vocabulary, and new actions - in short, a new way of living. We have to choose to surrender our lives to Jesus. As Jesus told his followers, *"if any man will come after me, let him deny himself, take up his cross daily, and follow me*
(Luke 9:23).

Do you ever see a tree struggle, strain or perspire in its attempt to bear fruit? Never.

The key to abiding in God's love is obedience to the Lord's commandments (John 15:10). The Word of God is our anchor. As Jesus said in **John 15:3,** *"Now ye are clean through the word which I have spoken unto you."*

When you live in Christ and follow Him with all of your heart all of the time, then you need not worry about how to be fruitful. The fruit will come naturally. God loves fruit and the more, the better. Just look at any healthy fruit tree. Do you ever see a tree struggle, strain or perspire in its attempt to bear fruit? Never - The tree merely has to have access to solid, fertile ground, sunshine, and rain. That's it.

Pruning

But that said, the Lord also tells us that God is *"the husbandman"* (v. 1) – the one who tends to the vine. He warns us that any branch in Him that does not bear fruit will be cut off (v. 2). On the other hand, every branch that does bear fruit He will prune so that it bears more fruit (v. 2). So prepare for the inevitable pruning, which ensures that there is even more fruit. Part of this process of divine pruning may involve self-denial and surrendering aspects of your current life to be obedient to God's commandments. Yet do not fear.

God's Secret Place

Hiding Place

Remember that the 'secret place' is also a 'hiding place.' As **Psalm 32:7** tells us: *"Thou art my hiding place; thou shalt preserve me from trouble; thou shalt compass me about with songs of deliverance. Selah."* When upset, trauma, or even danger is near, it is good to know that we can go to this hiding place and find safety. As we are beginning to learn, this secret hidden place is nothing less than Almighty God Himself. When we are abiding 'in God,' there is no need to worry. He is here with us and has everything under control.

Answered Prayer

Another bonus of abiding in God's secret place is that it holds the key to answered prayer. Abiding in Christ, while simultaneously having His Word abide in you, positions you to have big answers to big prayers. Ask what you want in accordance with God's will and it shall be done for you (John 15:7). Those who abide under the Almighty's shadow are protected and feel protected. They are permanently 'online' or connected with God. You can upload your prayer, praise, and worship, and He can download to you answers, blessings, and breakthroughs.

By contrast, if you are double-minded, with one foot in the world and one in the kingdom, you won't be able to enter into God's secret place. It may also cause you to risk being fruitless and outside God's protective perimeter.

The Promise of His Presence (v. 1)

As we are learning from **Psalm 91,** God is inviting you into His stronghold, which is nothing less than God's overarching presence. Whether you are in this world or the world to come and whether you are experiencing good times or bad times, there is nothing more precious

Three: Where is the Secret Place?

than God's presence. When God is with you and for you, nothing and no one can be against you (Romans 8:31).

The presence of God gives you courage and impetus to continue. Recall that Jacob was fleeing in terror from the wrath of his angry brother Esau (Genesis 28:15). There, at the special place called Bethel, God visited him and promised to be with him every step of the way in the pilgrimage of life. Whether Jacob was in the promised land or sojourning with Laban in Padan Aram, God was there. Twenty years later, when God called Jacob back to Canaan - and a further possible encounter with a vengeful Esau – God assured him, *"I will be with thee"* (Genesis 31:3).

The Benefits of God's Presence

Please consider that, amongst other benefits, the presence of God brings:

- **Courage in the battles of life**: Even if the opposing force is larger than life, you need not be afraid of it because God promises to be with you (Deuteronomy 20:1);

- **An incentive to keep going**: Moses faced the daunting task of confronting a hard-hearted pharaoh, but God's presence propelled him on (Exodus 3:12);

- **Greater closeness with the Lord**: This is because He dwells with you and you in Him (Exodus 33:14-17; John 14:20);

- **Rest and repose**: God's glory (*kavod* in Hebrew) is heavy but it brings rest (Exodus 33:14, 18);

- **Adoption and His superintending care**: You belong to Him and He belongs to you (Leviticus 26:12);

God's Secret Place

- **Comfort in trials:** Whether you are facing an ordeal by water or fire, God's promise of His presence will keep you from drowning or being burnt alive (Isaiah 43:2);

- **God among believers**: His presence is a cause of singing and rejoicing (Zechariah 2:10);

- **An incentive for fellowship**: When we gather in Christ's name, which means in obedience to His Word, under His authority, and according to His plan, we know that He will be present in that meeting (Matthew 18:20).

God's Omnipresence

As one prophet also discovered, once God has His sights set on you, it is impossible to escape from Him. This prophet was a man of God. But when called by the Lord to deliver a prophecy of judgment to a heathen people from a wicked empire, he chose to run from the Lord. Since God was known as the 'God of Israel,' the wayward prophet thought that the Lord could only be found in Israel. That meant that if he left the land of Israel, he also left the God of Israel behind, right? Wrong!

Maybe by now, you will have guessed who this prophet was. That's right, it was Jonah. He was called by the Lord to go east and preach to Nineveh, the capital of the cruel, war-like Assyrian Empire. Instead, he chose to go west to a place called Tarshish. Twice in **Jonah 1:3,** it says that Jonah travelled to Tarshish to flee *"from the presence of the LORD."* But Jonah discovered that God was present in the sea, in the belly of the big fish, and on the road to Nineveh.

God is present everywhere (omnipresent), as the psalmist also discovered in **Psalm 139:8-10**:

Three: Where is the Secret Place?

If I ascend up into heaven, thou art there: if I make my bed in hell, behold, thou art there. 9 If I take the wings of the morning, and dwell in the uttermost parts of the sea; 10 Even there shall thy hand lead me, and thy right hand shall hold me.

The presence of God can be a terror when you are running from or sinning against Him. After having disobeyed the Lord, Adam and Eve hid when they heard God walking among the trees in the garden (Genesis 3:8). According to **Revelation 6:15-17**, impenitent kings, great men, rich men, chief captains, mighty men as well as slaves and free men will hide from God's presence. They would rather have the mountains and rocks fall upon them than face God on His throne and the wrath of the Lamb. God is a consuming fire and His fiery presence will cause the wicked to perish (Psalm 68:2).

Having established the fact that God is present everywhere and that His personhood is a threat to unrepentant sinners, where does **Psalm 91** come in? God is ever-present with us. Yet the wonderful benefits we heard about earlier are only possible when we make a conscious choice to be present with Him: to dwell, abide, and remain in Him.

God Our Refuge (v. 2)

In **Psalm 91:2**, the psalmist makes a bold declaration that the LORD is his refuge and fortress. What might this mean? Let's focus on the refuge part. The word 'refuge' means:

"1. A place or state of safety from danger or trouble: e.g. David took refuge in the cave of Adullam (1 Samuel 22:1).

2. A place that provides a temporary home for those in need of protection or shelter."[iii]

God's Secret Place

A refuge can be a home, building, cave or island, but the main thing is that the fleeing person finds safety and peace in that place.

In Hebrew, the word for refuge is מַחֲסֶה *machaceh*. "Refuge or shelter from rain or storm, from danger, or falsehood" is used twenty times in the Bible (refuge fifteen times, shelter two times, hope two times, trust one time).[iv]

After a disastrous defeat on the battlefield with much loss of life, the remnant of the Benjaminites fled to the wilderness and stayed at the rock of Rimmon (Judges 20:47). When Saul the king sought to take David's life, David fled to the Cave of Adullam (1 Samuel 22:1). When Iranian students stormed the American Embassy in Tehran in November 1979, taking embassy employees as hostages, some of the hostages escaped and stayed at the home of the Canadian ambassador.[v] All these examples point to the same thing: when faced with great, even mortal danger, people seek a place of refuge.

But Scripture teaches us that the ultimate refuge is neither a thing nor a geographic location but Almighty God Himself.

Moses pleaded with God to show him His glory. God graciously complied. He picked up Moses and placed him in a cleft of a rock. This would provide a good vantage point from which to see God's splendour. At the same time, the Lord covered him with His hand while He passed by (Exodus 33:22). It is as if Moses simultaneously needed both a viewpoint and a protective place to shelter from the overpowering presence of the Lord. If we apply this in the context of **Psalm 91,** God will both elevate and cover His elect since He is their refuge.

Deuteronomy 33:27 speaks of the eternal God as our refuge. He undergirds us with his everlasting arms. Just as Moses got a lift up to the cleft of the rock, so too are we elevated. As we watch, the enemy will be thrust out from before us and destroyed.

Three: Where is the Secret Place?

God as refuge represents stability when even solid things begin to shake. The first three verses of **Psalm 46** imagine a time of upheaval which is so dramatic that the earth will be removed and the mountains will start falling into the sea. Yet, the psalmist declares, such a cataclysm will not trouble us because the Lord is *"a very present help in trouble"* (v. 1).

Fear of the Lord

The key to entry to God's superlative place of refuge begins with the 'fear of the Lord.' While we know that the fear of the Lord is the beginning of wisdom (Proverbs 9:10), what exactly does this mean? To begin with, it does **not** mean living in terror of God. On the contrary, it is to hear, obey, trust, worship, and serve God. **Hebrews 12:28** speaks of serving God acceptably with reverence and Godly fear. Similarly, we read in **Proverbs 14:26-27** that the fear of the Lord is a fountain of life to escape from the snares of death.

Another bonus of abiding is that it holds the key to answered prayer.

The divine refuge is multi-faceted. When we enter, God's strength will be imparted to us, especially to the weakest and most vulnerable in our midst. There is safety from the storm, a shadow in the heat, and a shield from the storm that hits the wall (Isaiah 25:4).

God Our Fortress (v. 2)

The faith-filled psalmist in verse 2 of **Psalm 91** proclaims that God is his refuge and fortress. Unless you have visited historic places such as the Old City in Jerusalem, you may be unfamiliar with fortresses, let alone how they can serve you in a modern context. In short, a fortress is a 'fort' or 'strongly fortified town.' The idea is that if you are in the fortress, you will be safe from external adversaries, even if they are very powerful.

God's Secret Place

Consider the life of David, King of Israel. He was well-versed in the notion of God as a fortress. So many times he faced mortal danger from innumerable enemies. Why? Because he was God's anointed (1 Samuel 16:10), David posed a threat to the forces of darkness. The trials he faced are graphically depicted in some of the psalms that he wrote. In **Psalm 18:4-5**, for example, David writes:

> *The sorrows of death compassed me, and the floods of ungodly men made me afraid. 5 The sorrows of hell compassed me about: the snares of death prevented me.*

Imagine facing this scenario day after day. But although Scripture speaks in detail about the life of David, nowhere does it depict him as having chronic anxiety or depression. This is because, despite furious and unrelenting opposition, he learned the secret that God was his fortress. He had first-hand experience of God's protection.

Speaking from a lifetime of dealing with danger and dodging death, David was able to affirm in **Psalm 18:2** that the living God was his rock, fortress, deliverer, strength, buckler, the horn of salvation, and high tower. So based on this, we too can say with confidence that God is our:

- **Rock:** He is a sure foundation, a pillar to lean on. When we build our life on Him, we will withstand all of life's storms;

- **Fortress:** The Lord is strong and fortified enough to protect all those who come within His care;

- **Deliverer:** As we will discover in **Psalm 91,** God may not keep us **from** trouble, but He will be with us **in** trouble. The end goal is that He will deliver us;

- **Strength:** Without divine strength, undergirded and upheld by the everlasting arms, even the mightiest among us will stumble and fall.

Three: Where is the Secret Place?

Fleeing to the divine fortress puts us in a position to draw on God's strength. When we are strong in God, we are strong indeed;

- **Buckler:** A buckler is a special small circular shield that fits around the arm. God's weaponry will more than a match and defeat the enemy's weapons;

- **Horn of salvation:** This is a figure of speech regarding God's infinite strength;

- **High tower:** The view is great from the high tower and there is complete protection. As we have learned, the Name of the Lord is that tower (Proverbs 18:10).

Consider the multitude of dangers David faced including those at the hand of Saul, the Philistines, Edomites, Moabites, Hadarezer king of Zobah, the Ammonites, Syrians, the Amalekites, Absalom, and Sheba son of Bichri. Yet David did not die at the hand of any of these adversaries; nor was he killed in any conflict. Instead, we are told that *"he died in a good old age, full of days, riches, and honour"* (1 Chronicles 29:28). Instead of perishing on the battlefield or in some palace intrigue (remember Absalom), he died peacefully in his own bed. Considering that his life was constantly on the edge, this was nothing short of a miracle.

How did he do it? God was His fortress. Let Him be yours too.

My God, In Him Will I Trust (v. 2)

Now that we have discovered the importance of having God as our fortress, we need a key to enter. The key is found in the following verse.

> *"Thou wilt keep in perfect peace, whose mind is stayed on thee: because he trusteth in thee."* — **Isaiah 26:3**

God's Secret Place

A few years ago, I had a conversation with a very smart Christian American who had a national radio program. This man was particularly knowledgeable about world affairs. After painting a grim portrait of the future, he was asked the question: "In light of all you have shared, what can we tell people to do to prepare for tomorrow?"

Without hesitation, he replied in just two words, "Trust God." He gave the correct answer. By coming to God, trusting in Him and obeying, you will quickly be ushered into His secret place.

What it means to Trust God

Everybody is trusting of somebody or something. In developed countries, people trust the post office to safely deliver their mail. Everyone trusts that the sun will rise tomorrow morning. Others trust that when they sit in the lounge chair, it will hold up their body. Retirees trust that their pensions will be deposited in their nominated bank accounts on pension day. All of these 'trusts' are fine, yet finite and flawed. Above all else, the most important thing is to trust God.

The Hebrew word for 'trust' is *batach*, which is used one hundred and twenty times in Scripture.[vi] It means to be totally and unswervingly confident in God. Examined from different angles, *batach* means to draw strength from the Almighty and surrender control to Him while you seek refuge in Him. Put another way, you allow God to carry you and your burdens. He does all the heavy lifting while you do all the trusting.

Benefits in Trusting God

The Bible lists numerous benefits in trusting God. These benefits are so remarkable that it is hard to understand why anyone would not wish to draw strength from Him. Here are a few examples of what we can expect:

Three: Where is the Secret Place?

- **No shame**: People who trust God may be ridiculed initially. But ultimately, they will never be put to shame (Psalm 25:2, 20; 31:1);

- **Divine Guidance**: When you lean on God in child-like trust rather than on your own reasoning mind, He promises to guide your paths like a good shepherd (Proverbs 3:6);

- **Everlasting strength**: Who wouldn't want to be stronger? Increased strength will help you survive and succeed in the days ahead. The secret to attaining everlasting strength is by trusting in the Lord forever (Isaiah 26:4). God is the source of all power, and the trusting believer is positioned to receive one great infusion of strength after another;

- **Prosperity**: Those who trust in God will be prospered or enriched (Proverbs 28:25);

- **Dwelling Place in the promised land**: This was the elusive goal of the Exodus generation. They left Egypt by the power of God but were marooned in the wilderness for 40 years. They never made it to the 'land of milk and honey' because they doubted God's provision for them. Instead, it was the generation born in the wilderness who received the blessing denied to their parents. Trusting God will take you out of Egypt, part the Red Sea, dry up the Jordan River, and cause you to enter and dwell in the land (Psalm 37:3);

- **A Place of Protection**: We learned earlier that God is our rock, fortress, deliverer, strength, shield, and high tower (Psalm 18:2). Trusting Him makes these attributes of God alive and active in our lives.

God is in Everything

Around 1870, a Quaker woman named Hannah Whitall Smith wrote a book called *The Christian's Secret To A Happy Life*. It sold millions of copies over the years and became a Christian classic.

God's Secret Place

Smith's thesis was that God is calling us to an interior life, the secret place of the Most High. Her main Scripture was **Colossians 3:3-4**, which states: *"For ye are dead, and your life is hid with Christ in God. When Christ, who is our life, shall appear, then shall ye also appear with him in glory."*

God is the source of all power, and the trusting believer is positioned to receive one great infusion of strength after another.

She also had what was regarded as radical ideas, including the view that 'God is in everything.' By this, she meant that no matter how difficult the situation, God is still sovereign. He is 'in it' and if you follow His principles, He will use adversity for your good (Genesis 50:20).

Surrender and Trust

Perhaps even more importantly, Smith offered two steps to achieve the interior life - the secret place. The first is **abandonment** or **complete surrender.**[vii] Instead of fighting circumstances, God or both, come and surrender all your concerns to the Lord. By doing so, you are passing on the problem to Him.

The second step is **perfect trust.**[viii] This means that your trust in God must be 100 per cent of your heart, 100 per cent of the time. This puts God in complete control of you and your situation. As already foreshadowed, this means that you become a candidate for answered prayers, breakthroughs, and miracles.

Try it for yourself. In practical terms, this approach of complete surrender asks you to trust God for every area of your life: Will you – can you - trust God for your finances? Your future marriage partner? Your family and friends? Your failures? Your future? If you can, you will experience strengthening and peace you never thought possible. You will be escorted to that safe space where God's presence, provision, protection, and power will see you through.

Three: Where is the Secret Place?

By now, we have discovered that the secret place of the Most High - the protective shadow, refuge, and fortress - is Almighty God. He is the goal, and trust gets us there. From this sure foundation, let us find out how we will be delivered from sin, self, and circumstances. It begins in the very next chapter.

.

---

[i] "H3427 - yāšaḇ - Strong's Hebrew Lexicon (kjv)." Blue Letter Bible. Accessed 19 Aug, 2022. https://www.blueletterbible.org/lexicon/h3427/kjv/wlc/0-1/.

[ii] "H3885 - luwn - Strong's Hebrew Lexicon (KJV)." Blue Letter Bible. Accessed 3 Nov, 2020. https://www.blueletterbible.org//lang/lexicon/lexicon.cfm?Strongs=H3885&t=KJV.

[iii] Courtesy of the Compact Oxford English Dictionary.

[iv] "H4268 - maḥăsê - Strong's Hebrew Lexicon (kjv)." Blue Letter Bible. Accessed 4 Aug, 2022. https://www.blueletterbible.org/lexicon/h4268/kjv/wlc/0-1/.

[v] The story is told in the 2012 American thriller film called *Argo* with actor Ben Affleck. The Canadian ambassador's residence proved to be only a temporary refuge. Had the Americans not moved on, they would have been captured.

[vi] "H982 - bāṭaḥ - Strong's Hebrew Lexicon (kjv)." Blue Letter Bible. Accessed 4 Aug, 2022. https://www.blueletterbible.org/lexicon/h982/kjv/wlc/0-1/.

[vii] Hannah Whitall Smith, *The Christian's Secret to a Happy Life,* Bristol UK: White Tree Publishing, 2017, p. 33 (Kindle edition). Smith's thesis on complete abandonment/surrender and perfect trust is found throughout the book but is mentioned explicitly on this page.

[viii] Ibid.

CHAPTER FOUR

Promise of Deliverance

Surely he shall deliver thee from the snare of the fowler, and from the noisome pestilence - **Psalm 91:3.**

Deliverance from Life's Traps and Pestilence

Verse 3 promises deliverance from the *"snare of the fowler"* (or hunter) and *"the noisome* [deadly] *pestilence."* These phrases may use archaic language, but they are metaphors for the pitfalls and challenges that we still face in modern times. The hunter's snare and the deadly pestilence extend into two realms of life: the physical, visible realm; and the unseen yet ever-powerful spiritual realm.

Life in this fallen world can be full of danger, and we have to make choices daily about how we conduct ourselves and about the company we keep. Whether through immaturity, folly, or involvement in an unfortunate situation, we can be drawn into activities that are contrary to God's design for righteous living. If we lack discernment and courage of conviction, we could easily find ourselves caught up in harmful or unlawful behaviour such as alcohol or drug abuse, sexual impropriety, pornography, or crimes of violence and dishonesty. We need to know how to avoid the hunter's trap, and as we will see, Psalm 91 leads the way.

God's Secret Place

Avoiding Traps

The book of Proverbs – written by King Solomon - contains a manual for good living. Twice it warns us that:

A prudent man foreseeth the evil, and hideth himself: but the simple pass on, and are punished - **Proverbs 22:3; 27:12.**

But despite this, Scripture also offers several examples where men anointed by God have made ill-considered choices at great expense to themselves or others. King Solomon - a man renowned for his wisdom - ignored God's directive to the children of Israel that they should not marry women from pagan nations, and this caused his heart to turn away (1 Kings 11:1-3). Consider also King David – a "man after God's own heart" (1 Samuel 13:14) - who fell prey to adultery and murder (2 Samuel 11-12).

Another allegorical but cautionary tale in **Proverbs 7** reminds us that we are all at risk from the stratagems of the enemy, no matter how strong we believe ourselves to be. We must always be on guard. The story relates to an anonymous *"young man void of understanding"* (v. 7), who goes out *"in the black and dark night"* (v. 9) and is seduced by a woman into an adulterous liaison.

As the story unfolds, we see the guile and determination of the adversary who *"lieth in wait at every corner"* (v. 12) and uses flattery to achieve his goal. So we are told that the woman, *"[w]ith her much fair speech ... caused [the young man] to yield,[and] with the flattering of her lips she forced him"* (v. 21). He didn't just go straight to her bedroom; he was headed directly towards his destruction just *"as a bird hasteth to the snare, and knoweth not that it is for his life"* (v. 23). It was a terminal encounter.

Four: Promise of Deliverance

What's even more troublesome is that we learn that the dangerous woman had a track record of conquests: *"For she hath cast down many wounded: yea, many strong men have been slain by her"* (7:26).

Another trap is the fear of death. This can be so debilitating that it brings bondage and capitulation to those who threaten. When you are controlled by such fear, you are easily manipulated and live under a heavy cloud.

And let's not forget the invisible yet powerful spiritual forces. Again, we refer to **Ephesians 6:12**, which tells us that our enemies include *"principalities ... powers ... the rulers of the darkness of this world, [and] spiritual wickedness in high places."*

Escaping Pestilence

Avoiding traps is just one challenge. The other one is escaping pestilence. Despite advances in modern medicine, it is still possible for people to be vulnerable to all kinds of illnesses, infirmities, or diseases. Epidemics and pandemics are now a very real possibility. Some diseases may also be caused by our own poor or even wrongful choices.

While we can take care to build up our immunity and avoid unhealthy lifestyle habits, let us remember that, ultimately, we need God to keep us safe and healthy. We can take all the precautions we want, but there is no way we can control all situations. Life is simply too big and complex for all that. Fortunately, the Lord is more than willing to provide protection and deliverance if we seek to abide in Him.

Deliverance Dispatched

Psalm 91 offers protection and deliverance in both the physical and spiritual realms and provides a way out and a way forward. The first word used in verse 3 - *"surely"* – confirms this.

God's Secret Place

God's willingness and power to deliver are evident in the Bible. Despite waves of trouble, Israel knew first-hand how God protected His people. They started in Egypt and the house of bondage. Then powerful signs and wonders, including the ten plagues, brought about their exodus from Egypt (Joshua 24:17). The journey to Canaan was long, but the nation remained intact because God preserved His people.

Biblical heroes like Jacob, Moses, Joshua, Gideon, Jephthah, Samson, David, Hezekiah, Esther and others were also delivered from great danger.

David, as king, embarked on many military ventures. He engaged with the Philistines, Moabites, Arameans, and the king of Zobah. Eventually, David enjoyed a temporary occupation of the world's oldest city, Damascus. Whatever he did and wherever he went, the Lord preserved him (2 Samuel 8:6). The reason should not be hard to figure out. David was a man after God's own heart (Acts 13:22), who spent time in His presence, knew the secret place all too well, and enjoyed the victories that followed.

In **Job 5:19**, we also read that *"[God] shall deliver thee in six troubles: yea, in seven there shall no evil touch thee."* This is a great statement of faith: God will deliver you in one or more troubles, one by one, or all together. As a bonus, you get the seventh deliverance, and no evil will touch you.

The New Testament and Divine Deliverance

The New Testament provides even more insight on the subject of deliverance. While we may be tempted to think we are the only ones facing affliction, the truth is that many others have already experienced this or will face the same thing in the future. Similarly, when temptation comes along, remember that according to **1 Corinthians 10:13**, you are only facing what many others also face. It is widespread.

Four: Promise of Deliverance

Amid the trial, God's faithfulness will be on display. You will not suffer beyond what you can handle. Indeed, God gives an escape hatch, promising that you will be able to handle the situation by His grace (1 Corinthians 10:13). During temptation, people can be purified by prioritising what is essential; they receive empowerment when they feel weakest; and then they see the miraculous hand of God for a breakthrough.

The God of all comfort is ready to deliver us from *"the sentence of death in us"* (2 Corinthians 1:9). Because He has done so in the past, we can and should have confidence in His future deliverance too. As the apostle Paul observes:

> *[T]he Lord shall deliver me from every evil work, and will preserve me unto his heavenly kingdom: to whom be glory for ever and ever. Amen.* (2 Timothy 4:18)

At the end of his life, in his last recorded words, Paul wrote that God had delivered him from *"the mouth of the lion"* (v.17). He went on to say that God would deliver him *"from every evil work"* (v. 18).

Though tradition says that Paul was executed by beheading, this did not separate him from the love and glory of God. On the contrary, his death propelled him into the presence of God. He wanted to *"depart, and to be with Christ; which is far better"* (Philippians 1:23); and following his death, he became *"absent from the body"* and *"present with the Lord"* (2 Corinthians 5:6). Paul was confident that he would be **delivered** from every evil work and **preserved** for God's heavenly kingdom. The great apostle had no doubts that he would arrive safely at the other side.

Preservation of the Saints

Life has enormous pressures, sometimes so intense that you may think that you will be unable to withstand them. Yet remember the principle of the diamond. We are told that its inner strength is so great that external pressure cannot break it. Those who dwell in God's secret place are His special treasure, and He wants to make you unbreakable too. It is part of His power to preserve.

People (or communities) who are still standing after intense persecution or affliction command our admiration. Yet even if an individual's survival can be partially attributed to personal courage and perseverance, ultimately, it has to do with God. He is the One who preserves us from all of life's afflictions.

If you want to experience God's preserving power, remember to abide in the 'fear of the Lord.' This is the starting place. Those who fear God obey God. Those who live such a lifestyle will experience God's preservation (Deuteronomy 6:24).

If you want to experience God's preserving power, remember to abide in the 'fear of the Lord.'

In **Isaiah 49:8**, the Lord makes an incredible promise. At an acceptable time and in the day of salvation. He will hear us, help us, preserve us, and give a covenant of His earth-based kingdom. We shall inherit the desolate heritages. For our purposes, the key point is that those who trust in God and abide in His safe space will be preserved and gain a great inheritance.

Other promises include divine preservation for the faithful (Psalm 31:23), everlasting salvation for the saints (Psalm 37:28), and preserved pathways (Proverbs 2:8).

Protective Power

This world order, ruined by the fallen state of humanity, has rendered the earth a tough place to live. Admittedly, some nations and regions can

Four: Promise of Deliverance

be tougher than others. In the natural, what do we have to protect ourselves? In many places, people have security systems, fencing, alarms, gates, grills, and, in the United States, an abundance of guns. Some learn self-defence techniques. The affluent can employ security services, guard dogs, and armed guards.

The community at large has the police and military. All these are designed to offer a measure of protection, but there is no perfect guarantee. Stories come from some of the tougher places on the planet that fences, barbed wire, chains, padlocks, dogs - perhaps a dozen layers of protection - still could not keep out the determined thief.

In light of this, what can we do? Come in faith to the God who promises to deliver and protect you.

By referring to some of the concrete and often powerful imagery used in the Scriptures, we can learn a lot about God's strength and protective power.

God as the Good Shepherd (Psalm 23:1-3)

A shepherd who is doing his duty will feed, guide, and protect the sheep. The rod and staff are a source of reassurance and comfort that the shepherd is on the job and ready to act for the good of the sheep. That's why David the psalmist, who knew a lot about shepherding sheep and people, could confidently speak of God as his shepherd. Even when David walked in the valley of the shadow of death, he feared no evil.

The Valley of the Shadow of Death (Psalm 23:4)

David, who came from Bethlehem, often took his family's sheep eastward through the Judean wilderness, which leads to the Rift Valley and the Dead Sea. As he got closer to the Dead Sea, the valleys became deeper and the walls higher. There could be dangerous animals and venomous creatures nearby, unseen behind the rocks. The sun set quickly; one moment it was light, the next moment darkness.

So how did the psalmist David remain fearless in the face of all this? The Lord, his shepherd, was with him. Yet how did he know God was present? The evidence is overwhelming: God's rod and staff were his sources of comfort, and God met all his needs. He prepared a bed of rest for David in the green pastures and created a soothing environment beside the still waters. And there is more. David also received a restored soul; divine guidance; extra awareness of God's presence in the valley of the shadow of death; the prepared dining table; the anointing with oil; the overflowing cup; and the perpetual presence of goodness and mercy.

As a result, David's discovery of God and the secret place has become ours too because of the celebrated Twenty-Third Psalm. We can have faith that God is present, God is near, and God cares.

The Mountains

Mountains represent majesty and strength and can even be protective like a fence. If you visit the city of Jerusalem, you will see that it is ringed by mountains and valleys. **Psalm 125:2** tells us that *"[a]s the mountains are round about Jerusalem, so the Lord is round about his people from henceforth even for ever."* God, who is greater than any mountains, uses Jerusalem to illustrate that He is always near and He always cares.

The Wall of Fire

Our God is a consuming fire (Hebrews 12:29), and this metaphor also speaks of protective power. God promises that in the glory times, Jerusalem will be so populated with people and livestock that it will have no walls. No walls? Indeed. For God will be the wall of fire around the holy city and the glory in its midst (Zechariah 2:4-5).

Four: Promise of Deliverance

The Angels

One of the many means used by God to give protection to His people are the angels who minister to the heirs of salvation (Hebrews 1:14). All those who believe in Christ are heirs to salvation. **Psalm 34:7** speaks of God's angel encamping around those who fear the Lord. What is his assignment? It is to protect and deliver them. We may not always see angels (or we might but they will look like normal people), but they are very busy doing their work of protection.

Jesus made an intriguing comment in **Matthew 18:10** when He warned us not to despise or look down on little ones. This is because, in heaven, their angels are always beholding the face of God the Father. Yes, angels are on assignment.

Reliance on People rather than God

The protection offered to those who surrender their lives completely to God can be contrasted with the situation of those who prefer to rely on themselves or others. Scripture gives illustrations of Biblical characters who put their trust in people rather than in the Lord. For example, King Asa of Judah wanted relief from the harassment of King Baasha of the Northern Kingdom of Israel. So Asa emptied the treasury of Solomon's temple, gave the riches to Ben-Hadad, King of Aram in Syria, and asked him to attack Baasha. The plan worked - Ben Hadad attacked Baasha – and Baasha desisted from his previous activities against Judah; but Asa discovered that his plan was only a temporary remedy (1 Kings 15:16-22).

The Judean king was rebuked by Hanani the seer, who went to prison for giving a forthright prophecy. His message to Asa was that God was more than able to defend His people without the need to bribe foreign heathen kings. But as he pointed out, God would only protect those whose hearts were perfect towards Him. Asa's actions were called foolish, and the result was that the very carnal actions he thought would avert conflict would ultimately attract even more wars (2 Chronicles 16:9).

King Hezekiah of Judah was a vassal to the Assyrian Empire (better that than to be conquered and deported as happened to the ten tribes of the Northern Kingdom). One of the conditions imposed on him was the payment of an annual tribute. Hezekiah decided he didn't want to pay it, so he made an alliance with Egypt. The gist of it was that if the Assyrians came to punish him militarily for non-payment of the tribute, Egypt would come and fight with him.

After withholding the tribute, and with Assyria on its way to Jerusalem seeking retribution, Hezekiah looked over his shoulder, expecting to see the incoming Egyptian troops. But they did not arrive. So he and Judah were left to face the wrath of Assyria all by themselves. Only through divine intervention was Jerusalem saved (2 Kings 19:35).

The Ezra Example

By contrast, we have the example of Ezra the priest who wished to return to Judah from Babylon to help rebuild the walls of Jerusalem. The voyage was a hazardous one, but Ezra felt ashamed to ask for armed guards because he had told the Persian King that His God would protect his company. So he refrained from the request, choosing instead to fast and entreat God for their protection. Despite the dangers, God brought them safely to Judah (Ezra 8:21-23).

The lesson is simple: if you want divine protection, come to God and His secret place, and let Him and His angels work for you.

The immortal God can save you from mortal men, sickness, and dire circumstances. The sinless Son of God can save you from sin, sickness, danger, worldliness, the devil, death and hell. The Holy Spirit can rescue

Four: Promise of Deliverance

you from evil spirits, heresy, and all manner of evil. The Godhead is waiting for you.

Deliverance Unto Victory

Life has many challenges, some seemingly insurmountable. But God's secret place is not just a space to hide; it is also where we find divine solutions, though not always immediate or obvious ones. Some challenges are natural, others are spiritual, and then there are those which are a combination of both. Malevolent forces are all around. Discernment to identify the source and nature of the challenge is needed - and available – in the secret place.

Because we presently live in a fallen world, we can expect to face temptation throughout our lives which leads either to a trial of faith or seduction of character. While some people thrive in a crisis, trials and temptations are normally challenging for most of us. Sometimes, through wisdom, we can avoid the pitfalls, but even the wise and Godly will be tempted at some point. It is the nature of our age.

Of course, some people suffer trouble because of the wrong and foolish choices they make. At least in such cases, there is an understanding of **how** the trial came about. That's why we need Proverbs-style divine wisdom. It shows us how to ensure freedom from folly.

But some trials are neither the result of giving in to temptation nor making foolish choices. They are spawned by satanic activity at work in a fallen world. Job was the victim of such activity (see below).

In light of all the potential obstacles and pitfalls that we face, what do we do? By now, we should know. We go to God's safe space. He is our refuge, our fortress, and our God who will surely deliver us from it all. God is bigger than all these forces combined, much bigger, *"because greater is he that is in you, than he that is in the world"* (1 John 4:4).

God's Secret Place

But after we are in the secret place, what happens next?

In the secret place, we can watch God work. He knows how to deliver the Godly out of temptation while simultaneously reserving the wicked for punishment (2 Peter 2:9). We receive power to overcome every pernicious, spiritual force and all the power of the enemy. We also have confidence that *"nothing shall by any means hurt [us]"* (Luke 10:19).

Humility, Submission and Weakness

But going to God's secret place implies humility and submission. If we can practise this, empowerment will follow, thus enabling us to overcome the most formidable of enemies. That's because when we are weak, God builds us up in the secret place, and we become strong. In that position, we learn that nothing can separate us from God and His everlasting love.

Job understood that only too well. He is an example of a God-fearing man of integrity who faced multiple, major tragedies in a short period. When he sought answers from God, heaven seemed to be silent.

As far as we can tell, Job never did get an explanation as to why he suffered (though we are given some insight from the dialogue between God and Satan in chapters one and two). Yet at the end of the story, Job got something far better than 'answers' to his suffering; he got God Himself.

In four chapters, God answered Job from the whirlwind (Job 38-41). Job was overwhelmed with God's words and presence. He repented *"in dust and ashes"* (Job 42:6). Then, after obeying the Lord's command to pray for his three friends, known as 'the miserable comforters,' God gave Job *"twice as much as he had before"* (v. 10). He *"blessed the latter end of Job more than his beginning"* (v. 12).

Four: Promise of Deliverance

In **Romans 8:37-39**, we see a whole host of things that could separate us from God including death, life, angels, principalities, powers, things present and things to come. But thanks to the secret place and the presence of God it provides, our weakness becomes strength, evil brings good, and opposition becomes enablement.

Freedom from Fear of the Future

Jesus Christ conquered death so that we would not be afraid anymore (Hebrews 2:15). For the believer, death is not a dead end, but a doorway to God. We are absent from the body, but we are present with the Lord (2 Corinthians 5:6, 8). Jesus Christ is the resurrection and the life (John 11:25). When you lose your fear of death because you serve Him, you stop being debilitated by fear of an unknown future. Instead, you become bold and unstoppable. You will be willing to do things and go places you never thought possible.

For the believer, death is not a dead end, but a doorway to God.

This deliverance unto victory even applies at the very end of this age. The apostle John received, by vision, what we now know as the Book of Revelation. The Bible's final book tells us about the last days and the turbulent transition from worldly kingdoms to God's kingdom. It uses striking symbolic imagery and speaks about a host of evil such as the antichrist, the false prophet, the harlot of Babylon, and Satan.[i] Yet its references to God are three times as many, and its titles and portraits of Christ exceed those which are found elsewhere in the New Testament.[ii] Its description of God's victory and the glories of the heavenly Jerusalem make all of life's sufferings easy to forget.

In **Revelation 15:2**, we read of a sea of glass mingled with fire. There is a group of victorious believers standing on the sea with the harps of God. They triumph over the beast, his image, his mark, and his 666 number (Revelation 13:18). Their triumph is ours as well.

God's Secret Place

Yes, in the secret place, you will find God, His presence and, as you are about to discover in the next chapter, His truth. God's truth is God's unchanging words for changing times. Read on and discover the power of that truth.

---

[i] There are numerous references to this cohort of pure evil, including Revelation 12:9; 13:1-10; 16:13; 17:1,15,16, 19:2.

[ii] Kameel Majdali, *Alpha & Omega - The Beginning of the End: An Introduction to the End Times* (Second Edition), Melbourne: Teach All Nations, 2011, 189-90, 192.

CHAPTER FIVE

God's Truth Delivers

He shall cover thee with his feathers, and under his wings shalt thou trust: his truth shall be thy shield and buckler — **Psalm 91:4**.

War on Truth

In this chapter, we will learn about truth - God's truth - and its wonderful, protective qualities. God's secret place is a sanctuary for His enduring truth. Yet to appreciate it, we need to understand that there is currently a war on truth, and it is savage.

One of the key signs which point to the return of Jesus Christ to planet earth and the establishment of His kingdom is the corruption of truth. When asked about the signs of His coming and the end of the age, Jesus' very first words were these: *"Take heed that no man deceive you"* (Matthew 24:4). Staying free from deception and walking according to the truth should be the highest priority for us as believers. Deception leads to condemnation and death (Revelation 21:8), but believing truth leads to salvation and life (21:3-4). No wonder **Psalm 91** describes God's truth as a *"shield"* and *"buckler."* Take hold of it and never let go. It is your lifeline. We will learn more about this shortly.

One of the greatest dangers we face in our world, especially today, is the assault on truth. False ideologies have spread the notion that all truth is relative: you have your truth, I have mine, all truths are 'equally valid' and no one's truth is superior to another. This teaching can be distilled into some of the following ideas and concerns:

- We are told that our age is a 'post-truth age';

- Truth is relative; there are no absolutes (absolute truth applies to all people and all times);

- This mindset has led to a proliferation of lying, spin, half-truths, fake news, and perjury;

- Of special concern is false witness, which is a serious violation of the ninth commandment (Exodus 20:16; 23:1);

- New and virulent strains of falsehood are rampant, including disinformation campaigns, gaslighting, and double-speak;

- People are becoming more experienced at lying convincingly;

- Even when you see and hear something clearly, you will be told you didn't really see this or hear that. This persuasive lying could make you doubt your sanity; and

- When presented with irrefutable facts and evidence, the post-truth person rejects it in favour of their chosen narrative.

The danger is that no civilisation can continue to stand if based on continuous and unrelenting falsehood. In addition, the eternal consequences of lying are dire (Revelation 21:8).

It is not that lying is anything new. It has been around since the serpent deceived Eve in the Garden of Eden. What is new is the expansion of lying across the board. In addition, it is not only your normal, work-a-day lying that will dominate in the last days. It is a spirit of deception and strong delusion, as we are about to see.

Five: God's Truth Delivers

The apostle Paul reiterates this exact warning, also in the context of the last days (2 Thessalonians 2:3). In **2 Thessalonians 2:9-12**, he speaks in sobering terms of the coming of the wicked one, also known to the world as the antichrist:

Even him [the antichrist], *whose coming is after the working of Satan with all power and **signs and lying wonders**, And with **all deceivableness** of unrighteousness in them that perish; because they **received not the love of the truth, that they might be saved**. And for this cause God shall send them **strong delusion**, that they should **believe a lie:** That they all might be damned who believed not the truth, but had pleasure in unrighteousness* (emphases mine).

Here is an important admonition. Even though the devil and his minions are working overtime to lie, deny, and deceive, God still commands us to avoid being deceived (2 Thessalonians 2:3). Should we allow ourselves to be led astray, it is we –not the devil - who will be held responsible because we have been exposed to God's truth, and He expects us to use it.

God versus Devil: Truth versus Lies

If you want a succinct and clear explanation of the source of lies and their adverse effect on truth, look no further than the words of Jesus Christ Himself. In **John 8:43-45**, Jesus confronted His enemies in an acrimonious exchange about the link between the devil, falsehood, and even murder.

Why do ye not understand my speech? even because ye cannot hear my word. 44 Ye are of your father the devil, and the lusts of your father ye will do. He was a murderer from the beginning, and abode not in the truth, because there is no truth in him. When he speaketh a lie, he speaketh of his own: for he is a liar, and the father of it. 45 And because I tell you the truth, ye believe me not (John 8:43-45).

God's Secret Place

From these verses in **John 8**, we gain much insight into the devil. He has evil desires and lusts, which, of course, is equally true of fallen humanity. Like Cain, son of Adam and Eve, the devil was a murderer from the beginning. The genesis of murder is an attitude of lies and hatred.

In the culture wars, the spirit of hate should be easily identifiable, in part because there is so much of it. When you hate something or someone so much, wanting to destroy them socially and culturally is only a few degrees away from wanting to destroy them physically and spiritually. Jezebel would be impressed.

From hatred and murder comes the devil's speciality: lies. He cannot handle the truth because he is utterly devoid of it. Lies are the devil's native language and representative of his entire nature. Death, murder, and lies are all linked and part of the devil's armoury.

God's secret place is a sanctuary for His enduring truth.

Then Jesus went a step further. He told the Jewish religious elite that they were the devil's children. The phrase 'son of' represents or suggests similar character and actions: like father, like son. Abraham's 'children' do what Abraham did; they respond in faith and become friends of God. The devil's 'children' emulate his actions: hatred, murder, and lies.

Jesus rightly accused His opponents of being the devil's offspring because they lied, believed lies, and had murderous intentions manifested soon enough at the cross. In addition, when confronted by genuine truth, they could not and would not listen. They rejected facts, reality, and even the gospel itself.

Of course, it is possible to go from being a child of the devil, full of lies, murder, and hate, to becoming a child of God. This transformation comes about by repentance from sin, faith in Christ, and obedience to His gospel. The penalty of guilt, shame, death and hell is banished.

Five: God's Truth Delivers

Forgiveness of sins, cleansing from sin, peace with God, the new birth, the fullness of the Holy Spirit, and the gift of eternal life are freely given to you. This is truly good news.

God's Supremacy

The secret place is a home for God's truth. You cannot know God's provision, protection, or presence without it. **Deuteronomy 32:4** tells us that "[*God*] *is the Rock, his work is perfect: for all his ways are judgment: a God of truth and without iniquity, just and right is he.*"

Lies are the devil's native language and representative of his entire nature.

From this, we can see that the contrast between God and the devil couldn't be more pronounced. One is from below and the other above. God is:

- **Omnipotent**: The devil has some power, God has all power;

- **Omnipresent**: The devil is present but God is all-present;

- **Omniscient**: The devil knows some things, God knows all things;

- **All-Good**: We know that while the devil is exceedingly evil, God is perfectly good;

- **Author of Abundant Life**: Whereas the devil devalues and steals life, God is the author of (abundant) life; and

- **All-Truth**: Whereas the devil lies totally, you can trust God to be the source of all truth (Deuteronomy 32:4; Psalm 31:5).

Unlike the devil, God is true, just, sinless, righteous, holy, and full of lovingkindness. God is confirmed as the creator of heaven, earth, the sea, and everything therein, and keeps truth forever (Psalm 145:5-6). If there is a human consensus about a story and God's view is the opposite, you can safely side with God every time. For He is faithful and true. We have the assurance that *"God is not a man that he should lie"* - **Numbers 23:19**.

The Three Sources of God's Truth

If you want universal, all-encompassing, everlasting truth, come to God. He is the source of it all. You will find God's truth in three distinct but related sources:

- First, Jesus Christ is truth personified (John 14:6). When Pontius Pilate asked Jesus, *"What is truth?"* (John 18:38), he had no idea that he was looking at the face of truth;

- Second, the Holy Spirit is truth (John 16:13). Indeed, He is known as the Spirit of truth. You can trust the Holy Spirit never to lead you astray;

- Third, the Scriptures, the Holy Bible, and the Word of God are the truth (John 17:17). The Spirit of truth inspired the writing of God's Word to bring us to God's Son, the Man of truth. You will never be misled by God or His Word.

If there is a human consensus about a story and God's view is the opposite, you can safely side with God every time.

We must acquire and maintain a high view of Scripture. To do less than this will hinder God's protective shield. We must believe that all scripture, not just some of it, *"is given by inspiration of God and is profitable for doctrine, for reproof, for correction, for instruction in righteousness"* (2

Five: God's Truth Delivers

Timothy 3:16). Similarly, **Proverbs 30:5** affirms that *"every word of God is pure: he is a shield unto them that put their trust in him."*

Jesus' view of Scripture was so high that He said that every letter and part of the letter was inspired and inviolate (Matthew 5:18). God's Word is all-pure, all-inspired, all-profitable, and all-true. His truth will be your shield as you put your trust in Him.

When you have all three sources of divine truth operating in your life - Christ, the Spirit, and the Word - you are in God's safe space. You are inoculated from lies and deception. You will be well-equipped to discern and reject falsehood, even if others embrace it.

God's Truth Protects (vv. 3-4)

The promise of deliverance from all danger is extraordinary, powerful, and true. In **Psalm 91:3**, we have seen that God will *"surely ... deliver."* It is a guarantee. Then the great psalm goes further and speaks of *"feathers ... wings ... shields ... and bucklers"* (v. 4).

What are these all about?

Of course, God is not a bird with feathers and wings. These are metaphors meant to paint a picture in your mind about an invisible yet powerful spiritual reality. Just as a mother hen or, better still, an eagle spreads its feather-coated wings to shelter and protect its young, so God does the same for those who trust in Him (Deuteronomy 32:11).

Remember that believing in God and His promises is a great start. But we have to go from faith to trust. Trusting God occurs when we practically, actively, wholeheartedly, and continually look to God for all our needs. Come to God and find a sure shelter.

God's Secret Place

God and truth go hand-in-hand. Where you have God, you have truth; where you have the truth, you have God. One of the secrets behind the relative success of western civilisation was its Judaeo-Christian underpinnings; and its commitment to the ten commandments, the rule of law, and respect for humankind made in the image of God. It is no coincidence that in a court of law, the goal is to hear 'the truth, the whole truth, and nothing but the truth.'

Shield and Buckler

In true Hebraic fashion, the Lord employs metaphors in Psalm 91 to show the power of truth and protection. God and His truth are likened to a "shield" and "buckler." A 'shield' uses strong material, held by a strap or handle, that protects from blows and/or missiles. 'Buckler' is similar: it is a smaller, round shield, which is upheld by a handle or worn on the lower arm. It affords added protection.[i]

> Jesus' view of Scripture was so high that He said every letter and part of the letter was inspired and inviolate (Matthew 5:18).

Like an intercessor, mediator, or advocate, God and His truth come between us and the enemy to afford cover and refuge from vicious attacks. God is *"our help and our shield"* (Psalm 33:20; 115:9-11). This shield/buckler protects and provides a great reward (Genesis 15:1); and it grants grace, glory and every good thing (Psalm 84:11).

Remember that the protective power of the "shield and buckler" comes from God's truth. We know that God's words *"are life unto those that find them, and health to all their flesh"* (Proverbs 4:20-22). But you cannot hope to stay safe if you entertain the spirit of this world (meaning the world system), the mindset of the world, and love of the world. **James 4:4** tells us plainly that *"the friendship of the world is enmity with God."* These are straight and strong words but true.

Five: God's Truth Delivers

God's truth delivers life. God's truth delivers from danger. God's truth cancels out deception. The sooner you embrace it, the better off you will be. And building upon this bedrock of truth, we are ready to learn how the secret place can deal a death blow to all fear.

---

[i] '*Buckler,*' Easton Bible Dictionary, Olive Tree Bible Software.

CHAPTER SIX

No-Fear Zone

Thou shalt not be afraid for the terror by night; nor for the arrow that flieth by day; 6 Nor for the pestilence that walketh in darkness; nor for the destruction that wasteth at noonday. 7 A thousand shall fall at thy side, and ten thousand at thy right hand; but it shall not come nigh thee. Only with thine eyes shalt thou behold and see the reward of the wicked.
— **Psalm 91:5-8**.

Facing Fear

As we continue our walk through **Psalm 91**, we are given a guarantee that may seem too good to be true: we are told that we will not be afraid of night-time terror, daytime arrows, pestilence in the dark, or destruction by day. These perils represent a variety of destructive methods and circumstances. Are the promises made in verses 5-8 simply poetic license and hyperbole, or can we take them at face value? Is it possible for life in the fallen world, headed towards its last days, apocalyptic climax, to become a 'no-fear zone'? The answer to this question is what this chapter is about.

A while ago, we took a flight from London to Amman, Jordan. As veteran air travellers, we understood that turbulence can happen during a flight. We also knew that it is usually more of an issue of comfort than safety. When you know where you stand (or, in our case, sit), you are better prepared when turbulence comes.

However, on this particular flight, nothing prepared us for what we were about to experience. The plane began to shake violently. My food tray was about to fly off the tray table. Coffee was spilling everywhere. Apart from an announcement to put on seat belts, the pilot offered no further commentary. This upheaval must have lasted from three to five minutes, with every second bringing an added measure of terror. Without question, it was the worst turbulence we had ever experienced. We wondered if the airstreams were going to knock us out of the sky.

My wife and I prayed passionately in the Holy Spirit (Jude 20), and at that juncture, we did not care who heard us. We needed to take hold of the Lord quickly.

Imagine going from a few minutes of turbulences to hours, days, weeks, months, or even years of it. How can we handle it? Well, God reassures us in **Psalm 91:5-7** that we do not need to fear anything. This is backed up by the wonderful promise from **Psalm 34:4**:

I sought the LORD, and he heard me, and delivered me from all my fears.

If the trial is strong, it is often proof that the person is too, and they become even stronger in the process. God is not tempting them beyond what they can endure. Hold on to this promise from God's Word - it will see you through anything.

Terror and Arrows, Night and Day (v. 5)

Thou shalt not be afraid for the terror by night; nor for the arrow that flieth by day - **Psalm 91:5**.

The fifth verse of **Psalm 91** makes a strong and assertive statement: you shall not be afraid. It is complete and unqualified. Then it outlines what you will not fear: *"the terror by night"* and *"the arrow that flieth by day."* As already mentioned, these phrases are probably intended to stand for or

Six: No-Fear Zone

represent everything that might strike fear in our hearts. There are further menacing situations mentioned in subsequent verses where the ability to terrorise will also be neutralised, but let's start with verse 5.

It is important to recognise that this verse is speaking about the occurrence of a miracle: freedom from fear whatever the circumstances may be. In this respect, Psalm 91 is not alone. Other psalms also speak about God's commitment to take you into a place where you are never afraid.

To appreciate the magnitude of the miracle promised, consider the great psalmist David, who faced death countless times and yet lived to old age. He was able to remain fearless in the face of catastrophic conditions: ten thousand people circling(Psalm 3:6); an enemy encamped against the man of God (Psalm 27:3); and an army launching war just on his account alone (think of Saul and his band of men seeking to capture David). Consider also the apocalyptic scene where the earth shakes and quakes, the mountains are tossed into the sea, the waters roar, and the mountains still on land shake like palm trees (Psalm 46:1-3). Yet we read that David simply did not fear. How is this possible? The answer is that David understood the importance of total reliance upon God. He had a lifetime of experience trusting God, and he had plenty of opportunities to put it into practice.

Trust and Confession

Scripture is replete with the exhortation to "trust in the Lord," and as we have already learned, the benefits of doing so are numerous. One of them is that you will be on an immovable, firm foundation, similar to a tall building with deep foundations, which might sway in a California earthquake but not collapse.

So out of a heart of trust, commit yourself to God, and rest in the fact that you are in good hands. The faith in your heart becomes the confession of

God's Secret Place

your mouth. David confessed that the Lord was his *"light and ... salvation,"* and *"the strength of [his] life"* (Psalm 27:1). Because of this, he had nothing to fear (v. 1).

Even when the wicked sought to destroy David, he neither feared nor lost his confidence. Part of this assurance came from the battles he had already won in the past. Though the enemy was powerful and well-armed, David witnessed time and again how these same foes stumbled and fell (v. 2). That's why life in 'God's secret place' includes confessions of faith in the One we trust and attesting to the victories He has already given us. David did both very well.

Seeking Proximity to the Lord

After trust and confession come 'crying unto the Lord.' This may or may not include tears and weeping, but it always means heartfelt supplication and/or intercession. Our actions at the altar of prayer should be genuine, whole-hearted, passionate, and to the point. We boldly come to *"the throne of grace"* where goodness and mercy are waiting to escort us (Hebrews 4:16).

If the trial is strong, it is often proof that the person is too.

Another way to view 'crying to the Lord' is that we are seeking proximity to Him. As the psalmist writes:

> *One thing have I desired of the LORD, that will I seek after; that I may dwell in the house of the LORD all the days of my life, to behold the beauty of the LORD, and to enquire in his temple.* (Psalm 27:4)

This is a wonderful verse to ponder, but the key is that David wanted to get close to God.

Six: No-Fear Zone

According to **James 4:8**, when we get close to God, He will reciprocate and come close to us. Yet the psalmist of **Psalm 27** was not content just to visit the House of the Lord; he wanted to dwell there for the rest of his life and forevermore. We see a similar desire at the end of **Psalm 23** where the psalmist declared that he would *"dwell in the house of the LORD forever"* (v. 6). When you are close to God and dwelling in His house, then how can you be afraid of anything?

Remember that the disciples of Jesus were also terrified when they were on the boat on the Sea of Galilee in the middle of a night storm, and the Lord was nowhere to be found. Yet He appeared, walking on the water, and got into the boat. Once that happened, the storm stopped immediately (Mark 6:47-52). The lesson is that when you bring Jesus into your boat, home, or heart, then you no longer have a problem; you have the solution. The same principle applies when you dwell in the house of the Lord - you are in proximity to God.

In words that echo **Psalm 91:5**, David confirmed in **Psalm 27:5** that *"in the time of trouble,"* God would hide him *"in his pavilion"* and *"in the secret of his tabernacle."* Not only would David be hidden from danger, but he would also be set high upon the rock. No storm of life was going to wash him away or steal his promotion.

The mighty armies and empires of the Bible have come and gone. The Egyptians were decimated at the first Passover,[i] and the Assyrian forces were destroyed at the siege of Jerusalem in 701 BC.[ii] Israel had every reason to be afraid but not when it trusted in God.

Night-time Pestilence, Daytime Destruction (v. 6)

Nor for the pestilence that walketh in darkness; nor for the destruction that wasteth at noonday - **Verse 6**.

If we practice trust, proclamation and prayer, it is remarkable how we can remain peaceful and calm in the face of challenges that would cause normally strong men to tremble. A third danger that menaces humanity is the pestilence that walks in the dark.

Pestilence that Walketh in Darkness

It is possible that the phrase *"pestilence that walketh in darkness"* is symbolic of every kind of evil that can wreak havoc in people's lives. But there is no doubt that pestilence in the form of life-threatening maladies or global pandemics can bring people and nations to their knees. In 2020, the world was hit by Covid-19, which caused governments to take unprecedented action such as closing schools, churches, businesses, and indeed, the economy itself. 'Lockdown,' 'mask mandates,' and 'vaccine mandates,' became household phrases worldwide.

There have been pandemics before Covid-19, but never has the world responded in such a way. One hundred years earlier, the deadly Spanish Flu Pandemic took place (1918-1920); it spread globally and took more lives in peacetime than those who died in the First World War. The death toll was estimated at anywhere from 25 - 50 million. Even back then, when people were dying in large numbers, it is unlikely that governments responded in the way that those facing the 2020 pandemic did.

But perhaps the greatest threat in such cases is the fear factor. What if you or a loved one were to fall gravely ill and die? What if your business were to fail? How could you survive without an income? Fear of the unknown can be incapacitating for many. But as we are learning, Almighty God does not want His people to fear anything. The only fear we should have is the fear of the Lord. As Sinclair Ferguson says "The fear of the Lord tends to take away all other fears… This is the secret of Christian courage and boldness."[iii]

Six: No-Fear Zone

How Should We Respond?

Our human response is to do what we can to build up our immunity. This is sensible and has its place but, most importantly, we should invest in our spiritual lives. In doing so we are optimally positioned to overcome fear.

There are natural, common sense things you can do to become healthy and optimise your chances of resisting or recovering from disease and viruses. Such steps include:

1. A balanced diet;
2. Exercise;
3. Fresh air and sunshine to help build up Vitamin D levels;
4. Pure water and drink;
5. Peaceful living;
6. Prayer and fasting;
7. Vitamin and mineral supplementation;
8. Where necessary, seeking medical treatment and following the advice of your healthcare practitioner, which may include vaccination (itself a controversial subject, therefore, be led by the Lord).

While these are reasonable actions, it is noteworthy that the Bible says little or nothing about any of them as a physical benefit. When it comes to health and healing, the Scriptures link these to our walk with God.

For example, immunity from the 'plagues of Egypt' was due to 'diligently listening to God's voice,' 'doing what was right in his sight,' 'listening to his commandments' and 'keeping all His statutes.'

The promised reward was that God would not put on them the diseases of the Egyptians. For, as God, Himself declares, *"I am the Lord that healeth thee"* (Exodus 15:26).

God's Secret Place

Health and healing are linked to God's Word. Proverbs 4, for example, states that if you listen attentively to the Word, hide it in your heart, and don't let it depart from before your eyes, you will find life and health for all your flesh (vv. 20-22). Remember, however, that your welfare is also dependent on keeping your heart pure and upright for out of it flow the issues of life (v. 23).

Health, healing, and longevity are vitally tied to divine wisdom and the fear of the Lord. **Proverbs 3** highlights this wonderfully. Keeping God's commandments from the heart brings length of days, long life, and peace (v. 2). When you embrace wisdom and understanding, you get a triple portion: length of days is in wisdom's right hand, while her left hand bestows riches and honour (v. 16).

Think about what God offers: longevity, riches, and honour. Aren't these the things that the worldly and ambitious seek after? Yes, they are, but God is offering these very things to the people who know and put Him first. The same three-fold promise of riches, honour and long life is given in **Proverbs 22:4**. The price for these promises is humility and the fear of the Lord.

The promise of long life continues. When you seek wisdom and understanding and hear and receive God's sayings, the years of your life shall be many (Proverbs 4:10).

When you have the assurance of good health and healing and these continue year-in and year-out, then you have positioned yourself for blessing. You know where you stand and shall not be afraid.

Destruction at Noon

If the nighttime has its challenges, what about the day? What about noon? Normally, noon is considered midday, lunchtime, perhaps even 'siesta time' if that still be possible. You are halfway through a normal

Six: No-Fear Zone

workday. Sometimes, important business happens around this time: Jacob met Rachel at the well at noon (Genesis 29:7); it was one of three times of prayer (Psalm 55:17); darkness turns to noon when you make God's chosen fast (Isaiah 58:10), and it was at this time that Paul saw the light on the Damascus Road brighter than the sun (Acts 22:6).

Psalm 91 makes it clear that challenges can happen at any hour of the night or day. But we learn that even if great destruction, whatever its cause, happens in the middle of the day, your residency in God's secret place causes you to remain free of anxiety. Your eyes are not on the noonday destruction; they are firmly on God.

Invincibility (v. 7)

A thousand shall fall at thy side, and ten thousand at thy right hand; but it shall not come nigh thee - **Psalm 91:7.**

If we can abide in the 'No-Fear Zone,' **Psalm 91** will take us to a remarkable vantage point. We can see everything below, but what happens at the ground level does not affect us above. As Habakkuk affirmed, even in hard times, we can still *"rejoice ... in the God of [our] salvation"* because *He is "our strength, and he will make [our] feet 'like hinds feet."* And when we have *"hind's feet,"* we can walk on the *"high places"* (Habakkuk 3:19). He gives us agility and the ability to rise above the challenges we are facing.

In the hill country of Galilee, there is a place called Mount Precipice, near the Biblical city of Nazareth. This is the traditional site of the 'brow of the hill' where the people of Nazareth took Jesus with the intent of throwing Him down (Luke 4:29-30). This incident caused the Lord to move to Capernaum by the Sea of Galilee. Why stay in a place where the locals want to kill you?

God's Secret Place

On Mount Precipice, there is a panoramic view of the city of Nazareth from behind and the grand sweep of the Valley of Armageddon in front. Your mind may whirl when you consider all that lies before you: Mount Tabor; the mountains of Gilead eastward in the distance; Mount Moreh with the Biblical villages of En Dor, Shunem and Nain; the mountains of Samaria to the south; and the Carmel range to the west. This viewpoint offers a great setting for a lengthy Bible session.

As we ponder **Psalm 91:7**, the mountaintop perspective offers a lesson in contrasts. Down below are the activities and challenges of this world, including war, upheaval, riots, unrest, and a myriad of other crises. Yet from above, we can see it all, but we feel safe and protected.

That's what verse 7 is about. Whether hundreds, thousands or ten thousand, no matter how many and in what circumstances, we need to trust that these adversaries will not come near to us. The key is to rejoice in the Lord and put on the hinds' feet (Habakkuk 3:17-19).

When you bring Jesus into your boat, home, or heart, then you no longer have a problem ... you have the solution.

Immunity for the chosen that is not available to the general population is not uncommon in Scripture. To the faithful, God promises that they will inherit the land if they wait on the Lord. With their eyes, they will see the reward of the wicked (Psalm 37:34), but judgment will not come near them.

Remember the ten plagues of Egypt in the days of Moses? In every situation, thanks to Pharaoh's hardened heart, the people of Egypt were afflicted by plague after plague. Yet the children of Israel remained untouched, even though they dwelt in the same land. The biggest exemption from judgement was their protection from the plague of the death of the firstborn. It affected everyone from the firstborn of Pharaoh who sat on his throne, to the firstborn of the servants and slaves (Exodus

Six: No-Fear Zone

11:5). Even the firstborn of the animals were slain. But even here, the Israelites remained untouched. They saw the curse with their eyes, but it did not come near them.

Israel's Protection as a Nation

From the Israelites' perspective, perhaps the greatest immunity of all is their continued existence as an easily recognisable people. According to **Jeremiah 31:35-37**, God committed Himself to preserve the people of Israel as long as there is a sun, moon and stars.

If you know anything about Jewish history, this is a miracle. For millennia, the Jewish people have remained a vulnerable minority, menaced with the twin threat of assimilation and annihilation. Yet while greater nations and empires have come and gone, the Jews remain until now. Where are the Philistines, Moabites, Ammonites and Edomites? When asked by a sceptical King Louis XIV for proof of the supernatural, philosopher Blaise Pascal (1623-1662) gave an eight-word answer: "Why, it's the Jews, Your Majesty. The Jews."[iv]

In his essay, *Concerning the Jews*, American author Mark Twain wrote these words: "*All things are mortal but the Jew; all other forces pass, but he remains. What is the secret of his immortality?*"[v] Again, **Jeremiah 31:35-37** provides the definitive answer.

New Testament and Other Examples

While these examples of immunity have come from the Old Testament, Jesus implies the same when giving the Great Commission. In **Mark 16:18**, He declared that those who believe "*shall take up serpents; and if they drink any deadly thing, it shall not hurt them; they shall lay hands on the sick, and they shall recover.*" Now we can treat this verse as a 'figure of speech' or accept it at face value.

God's Secret Place

One incident where Jesus' words came to pass occurred when Paul and his fellow travellers to Rome were shipwrecked on the island of Malta en route. It was cold and rainy so they made a fire, and Paul gathered a bunch of sticks. A venomous viper came out of the heat and latched onto the apostle's hand. He calmly shook it into the fire and suffered no ill effects (Acts 28:1-7). That's both the serpent and deadly poison provision of Mark 16 covered. Of course, it is also possible to lay hands on the sick, and they shall be healed.

In 1986, there was a nuclear power accident at Chernobyl, Ukraine in the waning days of the Soviet Union. Land for miles around was rendered radioactive and too dangerous to inhabit or cultivate for years to come. Even in what is now Belarus, the accident polluted the land. However, it was reported that a spiritual revival happened in a certain place (whether before or after 1986 is not known). The land that hosted the revival was perfectly fine, though it was surrounded by radioactive territory.

There is a lesson for us in all this. People who dwell in the secret place of the Most High will not necessarily suffer the same fate as those who don't, even though the latter may live in proximity to the righteous. Our eyes will see the judgment and destruction, but it will not come near to us.

Let this be an incentive for you: pray to the Lord of the harvest for more labourers. Pray for the fire of the Holy Spirit to fall. Pray that people may have a hunger for God's Word and a thirst for the rivers of living water of the Spirit. As we do, the circle of immunity and blessing will grow.

Only with thine eyes - God's Justice (v. 8)

Only with thine eyes shalt thou behold and see the reward of the wicked - **Psalm 91:8.**

Six: No-Fear Zone

Using the concept of comparison and contrast, the Holy Spirit inspired the psalmist in **Psalm 91:5** to illustrate the future of the righteous and outline what lies ahead for the unrighteous. The righteous will enjoy one outcome while witnessing the exact opposite for the wicked.

The Lord God has many great attributes, which we see described in the Bible. Our worship of Him is based not just on what He has done but also on who He is. We know God for His love, mercy, patience, power, presence and more. Yet an equally important but seldom considered characteristic is His justice. God is just. Abraham affirmed this in his question: *"Shall the judge of the whole earth do what is right?"* (Genesis 18:25). The author of the epistle of James cautions us when he says: *"Behold, the judge standeth before the door"* (James 5:9).

A simple working definition of justice is that God rewards the righteous and punishes the wicked. The scales are evenly balanced.

Psalm 145:17 tells us that *"[t]he LORD is righteous in all his ways, and holy in all his works."* So God's justice is derived from His righteousness. If He were not just, neither would He be righteous. Paul calls God *"the righteous judge"* (2 Timothy 4:8).

God's righteousness is exhibited by His nature but also by His laws, which have alpine-high standards. Righteousness is exhibited by conformity to the law. God's justice is exhibited by calling people to account for their good and/or evil deeds using corresponding rewards and punishments (Psalm 89:14).

God rewards the righteous, and this will include crowns of righteousness and life (2 Timothy 4:8; James 1:12). There is also a retributive side to God's judgment. He will punish those who transgress (2 Thessalonians 2:8). For Him to neglect retributive justice would be a denial of His righteousness because God hates sin and evil, and those who walk in the fear of the Lord must do the same. **Proverbs 8:13** tells us that *"the fear of the Lord is to hate evil."* Since God is faithful to His nature and cannot deny himself (2 Timothy 2:13), His justice remains intact.

God's Gift of Salvation: The Gospel of Christ

While we should be thankful that God is just, we can also rejoice that He is equally merciful. This can best be seen from the prism of the gospel where we see that we cannot keep the spirit or letter of God's law, try as we may. The Bible is clear: apart from Jesus Christ, there is not a human, past or present, who has not sinned (1 Kings 8:46; Romans 3:23); at best our righteousness is as filthy rags (Isaiah 64:6). Even more confronting, we are told that *"the wages of sin is death"*(Romans 6:23). We are all on death row.

Our only way out from this condemnation and death is to receive the 'pardon' of the free gift of the gospel of Christ. He took sin and the penalty for it upon Himself on the cross, and His righteousness has been transferred to us (Philippians 3:9). Thus, God's just requirement of punishing the sinner is met; and He rewards the righteous by imputing Christ's righteousness into believers' hearts. It is a truly win-win' situation for all who believe.

A simple working definition of justice is that God rewards the righteous and punishes the wicked. The scales are evenly balanced.

Such wonderful news applies only to those who have said yes to the righteousness, justice, and mercy of God. What we learn from Scripture and **Psalm 91**, in particular, is that those who come to God and His safe space are in a place of salvation. Yet their lofty position does not exempt them from seeing the reward of the wicked. They will get a balcony seat.

These words are not intended to be flippant; they are written with great concern and with an attitude of sobriety. Just as the grand ship Titanic sank on its maiden voyage in April 1912 after hitting an iceberg, so too is

Six: No-Fear Zone

our world order headed for destruction. No matter how invincible it may appear, our world is going down and taking everyone with it. The only way of escape is via the 'lifeboat of salvation.' There is a catch though. We have to leave the stricken ship behind and board the lifeboat. Those who do will be saved, but those who don't will go down with the ship.

The gospel of Christ is that lifeboat.

Retributive Justice Promised

The warnings of retributive justice are found throughout Scripture, including the New Testament. When giving the Ten Commandments in Exodus 20:3-17, God warned that those who worship idols, by bowing down and serving them, will be visited with divine wrath (v. 5). Part of the reason is that idol worship affects the present and future generations. In the same verse, God also describes Himself as a 'jealous God ' (in Hebrew, *El kanna*).[vi] God, as the one true God, will not tolerate any competition; and those who needlessly depart from Him and worship other false gods will be judged.

Retribution from a just and righteous God is very slow in coming. This is because of His legendary patience, known as long-suffering. Truly, the just God is One who also delights in mercy (Micah 7:18). Yet eventually, the door of the Ark must close, and justice must be served. When it is decreed, God's justice will be swift, strong, paid in full, and irreversible. He will not be slack with those who hate Him (Deuteronomy 7:10).

The **Book of Hebrews** wisely exhorts us to pay careful attention to sound doctrine. It is to our spirit what nutritious food is to the body. **Hebrews 2:2** suggests that those who transgressed the word spoken by angels received a *"just recompense of reward."* This is referring to Old Testament Israelites.

God's Secret Place

From there, **Hebrews 2:3** then asks how we New Testament believers will escape if we neglect Christ's great salvation. It was preached by the Lord Himself and then confirmed by His witnesses. Salvation in Christ is great but will do us no good unless it is embraced completely and stored in our hearts.

There will be those who receive the 'recompense of reward,' namely eternal punishment. Then some will witness it, but it won't come near to them. Make sure that you are part of the latter company.

Justice Delivered

God is gracious, kind, patient, and merciful; of that, we can be sure both Biblically and from experience. Yet let us not forget that God is the righteous judge, and where there is a crime, punishment must follow.

This is basic justice. Of course, the punishment must fit the crime. With God, that is no problem. To Him and Him alone belongs vengeance. And He will repay (Hebrews 10:30) at the time and place of His choosing. His judgment will always be righteous.

The following are examples in Scripture of the wicked receiving God's justice:

- **Adonizedek** (Judges 1:7): Adonizedek mutilated seventy kings and he admitted as much. He was repaid for his deeds.

- **Abimelech** (Judges 9:24, 53-54): The son of Gideon and a harlot, Abimelech grabbed power in Israel, killed his seventy (half) brothers, and ruled with a rod of iron. He died an ignoble death, at the hands of a woman, for murdering the sons of Gideon, and their blood was laid at his charge.

Six: No-Fear Zone

- **Absalom** (2 Samuel 18:9-17): The rebellious son of David, who stole the kingdom of Israel, was repaid for his rebellion. Absalom was summarily executed and immediately buried with a very great heap of stones piled on his grave. His troops, bereft of a leader, fled to their tents. The rebellion was quashed.

- **Joab** (1 Kings 2:32): Though loyal to David, Joab was a loose cannon who wantonly murdered two men more righteous than himself: Abner, son of Ner, captain of the host of Israel; and Amasa, son of Jether, captain of Judah's army. David did not have the heart to deal with Joab directly so he passed on the responsibility to his son and heir Solomon. Though perhaps only 20 years old, Solomon - at the urging of a dying David - had Joab executed promptly.

- **House of Ahab** (2 Kings 9:21-37): Ahab and Jezebel were the most wicked of all royal couples in Israel. Queen Jezebel had the prophets of the Lord hunted down and killed. Ahab coveted the vineyard of Naboth. So Jezebel planned his murder (and possibly that of his sons too because they were the heirs) and then stole his property. Ahab's dynasty paid the price. Ahab died in battle. His son king Joram, was executed by the incoming dynasty of Jehu, and his body was tossed into Naboth's vineyard. Jezebel, the mastermind of the murder, was thrown out the window in Jezreel, trampled to death by the chariots, and the dogs did the rest. The woman who was once the queen of Israel did not even get a proper burial. Covetousness is the subject of the tenth commandment. It is so evil that it may even cause people to be willing to kill in order to obtain what they covet. That's why Paul calls it idolatry (Colossians 3:5).

- **Haman** (Esther 7:10): As prime minister of Persia, Haman almost succeeded in destroying the Jewish people just because of his hatred for one man - Mordecai. At his command the mass murder of the Jews was scheduled for the 13th day of Adar. But rebels and wickedness often can't wait. Just as the builders of the Tower of Babel impatiently

God's Secret Place

burnt the mud brick rather than let it sun dry, so Haman had to have Mordecai dead long before Adar. But his wickedness was exposed and, as punishment, he was hung on the very gallows meant for Mordecai. It, therefore, pays to remember the warning of **Proverbs 26:27**: *"Whoso diggeth a pit shall fall therein: and he that rolleth a stone, it will return upon him."*

Of course, there are other examples of righteous retribution exacted by God on an impenitent people. Again, let us not forget the ten plagues poured out on a hard-hearted pharaoh and his people, including the infamous death of the Egyptian firstborn (Exodus 12:29-30). The parting and closing of the Red Sea was a judgment (Exodus 14:22-31). Israel's conquest of Canaan was a partnership with Almighty God to judge the heathen atrocities of the Canaanites (Book of Joshua). The siege of Jerusalem by the Assyrians under Sennacherib in 701 BC and his unlikely yet miraculous defeat was a judgment too (2 Kings 19:32-37).

Retribution from a just and righteous God is very slow in coming.

The very last verse of that great Messianic masterpiece called Isaiah offers this sober prophecy:

> *And they shall go forth, and look upon the carcases of the men that have transgressed against me: for their worm shall not die, neither shall their fire be quenched; and they shall be an abhorring unto all flesh.* (Isaiah 66:24)

It takes a long time for God's righteous judgment to get to boiling point, but when it does, this is the result.

Our key verse in **Psalm 91:8** tells us that with our eyes, we will behold and see the reward of the wicked. The seeing will be ours but the penalty theirs. This is echoed in the story of the believing Gentile centurion in **Matthew 8:11-12**, where Jesus says:

Six: No-Fear Zone

{M}any shall come from the east and west, and shall sit down with Abraham, and Isaac, and Jacob, in the kingdom of heaven. But the children of the kingdom shall be cast out into outer darkness: there shall be weeping and gnashing of teeth.[vii]

Whether the guests at the heavenly banquet see the weeping and gnashing of teeth is not certain; but like the rich man and Lazarus (Luke 16:19-31), some will be in bliss while others will be in judgment, with a great chasm in-between.

Now that we have heard the bad news, it is time for some good news.

Repentance and God's Forgiveness

Judgment is, understandably, not a popular subject and, clearly, it is not for the faint-hearted either. Yet it is one of the fundamental doctrines of the Christian faith (Hebrews 6:2). Fortunately, eternal judgment is not inevitable. There is a way of escape.

While many in the Bible were judged by God and forfeited their lives, with their hearts still hard as stone, some repented and were forgiven, despite the gravity of their sin. David was one of them. Though he was rightly accredited as a man of God, a model worshipper, a highly gifted individual, and a shepherd to the sheep, he was not perfect. We see in **2 Samuel 11** that he committed serious sins and violated at least five of the Ten Commandments:

- **The Tenth Commandment - Covetousness** (Exodus 20:17): David coveted Bathsheba, the wife of one of his mighty men, Uriah the Hittite. This took place while his servant was fighting David's battle at Rabbah-Ammon (modern-day Amman, capital of Jordan). Once sin begins, it can often lead to other sins, much like standing on a slippery slope and losing control;

- **The Second Commandment - Idolatry** (Exodus 20:3-6): Covetousness is considered idolatry, as we learned already;

- **The Eighth Commandment - Theft** (Exodus 20:15): David took Uriah's wife - the result of covetousness. After all, it wasn't as if he lacked women in his life. Yet covetousness and theft are never satisfied since often they are not based on need but greed. The thief will want more.

- **The Seventh Commandment - Adultery** (Exodus 20:14): David was a polygamist, as were other prominent men in the Bible (Jacob, Gideon, Solomon, and other kings). Yet sleeping with Uriah's wife was an act of betrayal and treachery that was inexcusable, especially for a man chosen as God's leader;

- **The Sixth Commandment - Murder** (Exodus 20:13): After coveting and stealing Bathsheba (who became pregnant), David tried to cover his tracks by effectively having Uriah murdered in battle so he could quickly wed Bathsheba.

In mercy, God dispatched the prophet Nathan to confront the wayward king. The prophecy he delivered was stinging. Because David had taken the widowed Bathsheba as his wife in a 'shot-gun wedding,' the prophet said that he had despised the Lord (2 Samuel 12:10). What did Nathan mean by that? To despise means to show contempt, hatred, deep repugnance, or little regard for someone who deserves much more. Never forget that sexual sin is an offence against your own body, your family and, ultimately, against God Himself.

What was David's punishment? The sword would never depart from David's house. Amnon, Absalom, and Adonijah, all David's sons, succumbed to the sword (2 Samuel 13:28-29; 18:14-15; 1 Kings 2:24-25). David paid the price for his sin - one night of fleeting, sensuous pleasure - for the rest of his life. If he were here on earth, he would undoubtedly tell you: 'It wasn't worth it. Don't go there.'

Six: No-Fear Zone

It was not uncommon for prophets to face severe punishment, even death, for fearlessly delivering the word of the Lord to a backslidden monarch. Fortunately for Nathan, David responded positively and acknowledged that he had *"sinned against the LORD"* (2 Samuel 12:13). These words of repentance and regret are the beginning of hope. If you want to see David's full 'mea culpa,' read **Psalm 51**. It is a cry from the soul.

God's Mercy

When people humble themselves, the mercy of God takes over. In the same verse, Nathan responded to David's plea for forgiveness by telling him: *"The LORD also hath put away thy sin; thou shalt not die"* (2 Samuel 12:13).

The wonderful news is that God is gracious. Yet even though David was forgiven, the price of his sin still played out for the rest of **2 Samuel 1** and **2 Kings**. There were consequences for his wrongdoing. Again, friends, sin is not worth it.

Blessed are the Merciful

God's mercy towards us means that it is also important that we show mercy to others. There are many fine examples of people receiving mercy because they gave mercy. A merciful young woman showed kindness to the elderly. One of her beneficiaries predicted that because she sowed mercy in her youth, she would reap mercy in her old age. This prediction came to pass, and she spent her last years among family and friends, full of joy. She even died a good death - smiling, saying how blessed she was, then closing her eyes and departing. What a way to go![viii]

Another story involves a kind-hearted, Spirit-filled lady who helped assist an older woman in practical ways. She had no motivation except to demonstrate the love of Christ. Subsequently, the older woman died and left property to the 'mercy lady' in her will. She didn't expect it, but the proceeds blessed her in her retirement.[ix]

So take to heart the exhortation: *"Blessed are the merciful: for they shall obtain mercy"* (Matthew 5:7). If someone is down, don't kick them in the side. If someone errs, don't be harsh. If someone needs help, and you are in a position to assist, then do so (Proverbs 3:27-30). For to be merciful is to show love in the present and prudence for the future. When the time comes that you need mercy, it will be waiting for you. You will wonderfully reap in mercy that which you have sown.

The most compelling reason for us to show mercy is because of the mercy that we have received ourselves as believers. But it is our salvation that also gives us the greatest freedom from fear.

Freedom from Fear of Judgment

The price for sin - judgement - was paid in full by Jesus Christ on the cross. As Jesus said in **John 5:24**:

He that heareth my word, and believeth on him that sent me, hath everlasting life, and shall not come into condemnation; but is passed from death unto life.

If you repent, believe, and receive, you will be justified, not condemned, by God. You will pass from death to life. This is the ultimate mercy.

Through the gospel of Christ, God is offering to cancel the judgment and punishment that we deserve and to bestow on us amazing grace that we don't deserve. What better way to close this chapter than with the words of the most famous verse in Scripture – the key verse in fact - that describes what the entire Bible is all about:

Six: No-Fear Zone

For God so loved the world, that he gave his only begotten Son, that whosoever believeth in him should not perish, but have everlasting life (John 3:16).

Now that you have been introduced to the promise of fearlessness in **Psalm 91**, it is time to view the promise of divine protection with fresh eyes. The next chapter will show the way.

---

[i] Egypt was decimated at the first Passover by the death of the firstborn (Exodus 12:29-30) and the parting of the Red Sea (Exodus 14:13, 14, 30, 31).

[ii] The Assyrian forces besieging Jerusalem in 701 BC were divinely defeated (2 Kings 19:32-35).

[iii] https://gracequotes.org/quote/the-fear-of-the-lord-tends-to-take-away-all-other-fears-this-is-the-secret-of-christian-courage-and-boldness/ Accessed 5 August 2022.

[iv] https://aish.com/48964091/. Accessed 5 August 2022.

[v] *Quotes on Judaism & Israel: Mark Twain.* The Jewish Virtual Library. https://www.jewishvirtuallibrary.org/mark-twain-quotations-on-judaism-and-israel Accessed 5 August 2022.

[vi] "H7067 - qannā' - Strong's Hebrew Lexicon (kjv)." Blue Letter Bible. Accessed 20 Aug, 2022. https://www.blueletterbible.org/lexicon/h7067/kjv/wlc/0-1/.

[vii] After commending his faith, Jesus then told his followers that there would be Gentiles in the kingdom of heaven (a radical view at that time) but that not all Jews (known as children of the kingdom at that time because of their knowledge of YAHWEH) would necessarily be there.

[viii] The woman in the story is the paternal grandmother of the author.

[ix] The subject of this story is the maternal aunt of the author.

CHAPTER SEVEN

Divine Protection Reaffirmed

Because thou hast made the Lord, which is my refuge, even the most High, thy habitation; 10 There shall no evil befall thee, neither shall any plague come nigh thy dwelling - **Psalm 91:9-10**.

The Most High God (v. 9)

We return to some wonderful themes mentioned earlier in **Psalm 91**: God the refuge and God Most High. It is not uncommon for Biblical Hebrew to provide 'creative repetition' by mentioning something again but giving additional information. Since these points are fundamental, hearing them again consolidates the message but also inspires us.

As we have already learned, God the Most High (*El Elyon*) means He is beyond peer. God's nature, position, thoughts, and actions are demonstrably higher, more righteous, and superior in every way to the thoughts and ways of humanity. While there are philosophies and ideologies with a kernel of truth, God provides all truth. Militarily, there are some mighty nations, but God is Almighty and omnipotent.

From every vantage point, the truly wise person comes close to God by walking in the fear of the Lord. Yet presumptuous humanity often thinks it knows better than Almighty God Himself. But no matter how educated or wise an individual may be naturally, only a foolish person avoids, scorns, or rejects God's teachings. Let us remind ourselves of the powerful words from the prophet Isaiah:

God's Secret Place

For my thoughts are not your thoughts, neither are your ways my ways, saith the LORD. For as the heavens are higher than the earth, so are my ways higher than your ways, and my thoughts than your thoughts. (Isaiah 55:8-9)

God's Almighty-ness

Scripture is replete with signs of God's power and glory. When God speaks, His voice is so endued with power and authority that it is like thunder from heaven (2 Samuel 22:14). In fact, God's voice is so majestic and powerful that we are told it breaks the cedars of Lebanon (Psalm 29:5). When God spoke with an audible voice out of heaven (John 12:28-30), the people couldn't decide whether it was thundering or an angel was speaking. So awesome is God Almighty's voice that even the dead shall hear it and come forth out of their graves in the future (John 5:28-29).

God's Position

The Most High God doesn't just have a powerful voice; He also holds a powerful position as Sovereign of the universe. This is confirmed repeatedly in Scripture where God is declared to be:

- *"[T]errible"* and *"a great King over all the earth"* (Psalm 47:1-2). Note here that the word 'terrible' doesn't mean what it means today. Its real meaning is found in the New King James Version where it is translated as *"awesome"*;

- *"Most high over all the earth "* (Psalm 83:18).

When speaking to the ruthless king Nebuchadnezzar, potentate of the greatest of ancient empires, Daniel the prophet informed him that there was an even greater power than him: *"The most High ruleth in the kingdom*

Seven: Divine Protection Reaffirmed

of men, and giveth it to whomsoever he will" (Daniel 4:17). Amazingly, this difficult, proud, and arrogant monarch did get the message (v. 37).[i]

Similarly, in **Revelation**, as the unveiling of God's prophetic plan began, John was told that Jesus Christ, Son of the Most High, is the prince/ruler of the kings of the earth (1:5).

Since God is supreme, there is no power, potentate, president or prime minister who is above Him. He is the Head of all (although it may not seem to be that way with the proliferation of ungodliness on the earth today). But don't be fooled. He can raise up powers and remove powers at any time He so desires (Daniel 2:21). Without a doubt, God is on the throne and His kingdom is coming.

Our Response to God

If we are to enjoy the privileges and benefits of **Psalm 91**, we need to be reminded again and again of the nature of the God who provides them. Given God's exalted position as God Most High, we must also know how to respond to Him. Once more, Scripture is our guide. David said he would praise God according to His righteousness (Psalm 7:17). How righteous is God Most High? Immeasurably so. The praise should, therefore, be generous, whole-hearted, sincere, and ongoing (Psalm 92).

As the Lord is Sovereign of the universe, there is no power, potentate, president or prime minister who is above Him.

Both psalmists in **Psalm 7** and **Psalm 92** also say that they will sing their praises to the name of the Lord Most High (7:17; 92:1). You don't need a concert-quality voice to sing praise to God; you just need to have a voice and a single heart.

There's still more: the sons of Korah exhort God's people to clap their hands and shout to God with the voice of triumph (Psalm 47:1-2). It is

God's Secret Place

customary to think that we should be quiet and reverent in the presence of God - and there is a place for that. However, there is solid Biblical evidence that God-pleasing praise and worship were anything but a quiet event. God's throne is not like a hushed public library or morgue; it is a place of glorious and intent spiritual activity. Heaven is not a subdued place (and, for the matter, neither is hell).

God My Refuge (v. 9)

Because thou hast made the Lord, which is my refuge, even the most High, thy habitation - **Psalm 91:9**.

Verse 9 offers a further reminder that the Lord is the Most High God and that His authority and position mean that we have access to everything we need. If we make our habitation in and with Him, then we find the safest refuge of all - God's safe space.

We find the same promises in Isaiah where God declares:

[M]*y people shall dwell in a peaceable habitation, and in sure dwellings, and in quiet resting places.* (**Isaiah 32:18**)

God's Workshop

What may not be so apparent is that the refuge - the place where our *"life is hid with Christ in God"* (**Colossians 3:3**) - is a workshop for God to do His great work in our lives. In other words, the refuge is not just a place to hide; it is a place of help - divine help.

A good example of this is found in **Psalm 121:2-4**. These three verses cover a range of information. The Creator God, who made heaven and earth, is in the business of helping. The Lord provides round-the-clock security because He neither slumbers nor sleeps. Not only are the big issues under His watchful eye but He will also keep your every step in

Seven: Divine Protection Reaffirmed

line. In addition, the very hairs of your head are all numbered (Matthew 10:30), and God knows you by name (John 10:3). That's how meticulous His care is.

Inside the divine refuge, God will calm you, load you with His peace (John 14:27), and keep you from the fear of evil (Proverbs 1:33). By day, you will walk in a sure-footed and confident manner; by night, you can lie down, easily fall asleep (Proverbs 3:23-24), and enjoy sweet dreams.

Israel's Security

Ancient and modern Israel is located at the navel of the world - the land bridge between Africa and Eurasia. This tiny postage stamp of land is the link between the continents and the great powers of old: Egypt, Assyria, Babylon, Persia, Asia Minor, and Imperial Rome. At any time, larger nations and empires could march through without warning or permission. God positioned His covenant people in such a place, not to make them vulnerable and insecure but so that they would learn to have whole-hearted dependence on Him. Because God was their refuge and fortress, they saw (and will see again) that God is greater than any earthly power.

The time is coming when Israel will no longer be at the mercy of the great powers. In **Jeremiah 23:6**, we are told that *"Judah shall be saved and Israel dwell safely,"* and we know this because the divine helper is the divine keeper (Psalm 121:4-5).

When will Israel live in complete security? When Jesus returns to this planet, He will sit on the throne of David in Zion (Psalm 2). Judah and Israel will be reunited under the Messiah Jesus, the Son of David/Son of God. He will be known as *"THE LORD OUR RIGHTEOUSNESS"* (Jeremiah 23:6).

God's Secret Place

Righteousness comes from God

Just as the Lord is righteous, we too can and must be righteous. True righteousness does not come from human effort and ingenuity; it comes from God and is transferred into our hearts by faith (Philippians 3:9).

Once we have taken this step, then refuge, security, divine help, and safety are the prizes we get for making the Lord our God an eternal refuge. It is in this context that we can take a fresh look at the promise that God will never leave us nor forsake us. How can He do so when we make our habitation in Him? Yet if we live our lives in self-will and spurn God's will, then even though He may be 'near,' He won't necessarily be 'here' with us.

This fallen world we live in is a tough sinful place, which will be restored one day. But in the meantime, it is best to head to the divine refuge. God's presence is guaranteed and will make you fearless. With the Lord as *"[your] helper,"* there is no need for you to *"fear what man shall do unto [you]"* (Hebrews 13:6).

The Epistle of 1 Peter was written to the suffering church to encourage it. In **1 Peter 3:13-15**, we are exhorted to count ourselves happy if we suffer for righteousness' sake; and not to be afraid or troubled by our persecutors or fearful of their threats. Yet that same passage assures us that the Lord watches over the righteous, and His ears hear their prayers. Joy, vindication, and victory are only possible when God Most High is your habitation. Dwelling outside the divine precinct leaves you vulnerable, but living under the shadow of His wings brings you these supernatural blessings.

See No Evil (v. 10)

There shall no evil befall thee, neither shall any plague come nigh thy dwelling - **Psalm 91:10**.

Seven: Divine Protection Reaffirmed

Another supernatural benefit promised in **Psalm 91:10** is that no evil will come upon you and plagues will keep clear of your abode. These undertakings appear unconditional and without qualification. But despite this, we have already seen earlier that because we live in a fallen world, believers are not always exempt from pain and suffering. We also know that righteous people can expect to suffer because of their righteousness. If this is so, then what are we to make of this? And how can it be said that we are immune from evil?

This beautiful verse conveys the superlative promise of divine care, comfort, and protection to the people who put their trust in Him. So it is reasonable for believers to expect miracles and many do experience them. But we also get an answer later in the psalm. The key is that God may or may not prevent the evil from coming your way; but if it arrives on your doorstep, He will be with you in it. You are not facing anything alone. Furthermore, if you exercise your faith, you will eventually see evil overcome.

Yet if we live our lives in self-will while spurning God's will, then even though He may be 'near,' He won't necessarily be 'here' with us.

A story is told of an Asiatic cholera outbreak in London during the 1850s.[ii] The pastor had the weighty burden of visiting the sick, the dying, and the dead. There was funeral after funeral, all of which caused a heaviness bordering on despondency. Not only was there personal grief for those who were gone but also the feeling of personal vulnerability. The pastor asked: Will I, too, get sick? Will I even survive or will I succumb?

What do you do in times such as these? You come to God's safe space, as outlined in **Psalm 91**. The minister found a piece of paper posted in a shop window with these words written from **Psalm 91:10**: *"There shall no evil befall thee, neither shall any plague come nigh thy dwelling."* The effect on him was immediate. Faith rose in his heart since faith comes by hearing

God's Secret Place

and hearing from the Word of God (Romans 10:17). His mood and mindset changed immediately. The fear was gone; the heaviness was lifted; and the turmoil was replaced with peace.

The minister was able to continue his visitation to the infirm and dying with a new calm and confidence. He did not succumb to fear, and he did not get sick; no plague came near him or his dwelling. That's the power of the secret place of the Most High.

Experiencing Peace in Your Trial

You may not always get such a tidy, text box answer to your own frightening or difficult situations. But that does not mean that you cannot experience the same peace as the others. By now, you should know what to do. Keep actively and consistently committing your fears and problems to God; and keep trusting, praying, praising, and patiently enduring. You are serving God nobly as you continue to persevere in the face of trials. And your reward will be great.

How long should you keep 'trusting God'? As long as it takes. Continuous trust in the Almighty is your lifeline, and if you let go, you will be in free fall. If your eyes and hearts are open, you will see faith mileposts along the way. These are acts of divine grace to let you know that you are on the right path, heading in the right direction. Some of these mileposts may require a simple step of obedience; they are merely reminders to 'keep going' and 'keep trusting.'

While you seek God during the trial, ask Him if there are any sins in your own life you need to forsake. If so, recognise and repent of them. If nothing is brought to your attention, go to the next valid question: Are there any lessons God would have you learn? If so, try to learn them quickly so you can graduate to the next level.

Seven: Divine Protection Reaffirmed

As you heed the lessons in **Psalm 91**, you can take comfort from the fact that God will provide you with **effective** support. It can come in human or divine form. In addition, the Lord may send special, powerful assistants to help us along the way.

We will meet them in the very next chapter.

---

[i] This chapter is almost certainly the confession of Nebuchadnezzar, not the words of Daniel, though there is the possibility that the prophet instructed the king in this matter.

[ii] Spurgeon,C."Psalm 91 by C.H.Spurgeon. Spurgeon, C. "Psalm 91 by C. H. Spurgeon." Blue Letter Bible. Last Modified 5 Dec 2016. https://www.blueletterbible.org/Comm/spurgeon_charles/tod/ps091.cfm. Accessed 5 August 2022.

CHAPTER EIGHT

Angels on Assignment

For he shall give his angels charge over thee, to keep thee in all thy ways. 12 They shall bear thee up in their hands, lest thou dash thy foot against a stone - **Psalm 91:11-12**.

For those of you who abide in God's secret place, **Psalm 91:11** tells us that He especially commissions helpers to keep watchful charge over you. They are heavenly bodyguards, and more.

These helpers are angelic beings. Wherever you stay, they will stay, and wherever you travel, they will accompany you. Their assignment is to watch over the entire person: body, mind, soul, and spirit. And they keep you in all your ways, wherever you go.

Ministering Angels (vv. 11-12)

Angels are a feature in Scripture from Genesis to Revelation. While they are ever-present, they can be elusive, easily camouflaged, and misunderstood. Yet for those who seek to be in God's presence, angels are part of the package deal.

Here are some interesting statistics about the words 'angels' and 'angel' in the Bible:[i]

- **Genesis**: 'Angels' are mentioned four times; 'angel' eleven times. There was a lot of angelic activity *"in the beginning."*

- **Psalms**: 'Angels' are mentioned eight times; 'angel' three.

- **Four Gospels**: 'Angels' are mentioned twenty-nine times; 'angel' twenty-three times. The angels were working hard because Christ worked hard.

- **Acts**: 'Angels' are mentioned only once, but 'angel' twenty times. While the Holy Spirit was paramount in the birth and growth of the church, angelic activity was part of making it happen.

- **Hebrews**: 'Angels' are mentioned twelve times. Christ is described as better than the angels but, at the same time, we get more insight about them and their work.

- **Revelation**: 'Angels' are mentioned twenty-two times; but 'angel' is cited a massive fifty-one times. Since there was much angelic work in the beginning, it is not surprising that it also greatly intensifies at the end.

While God, as sovereign, can be involved either directly or indirectly as He deems fit, angels are God's servants with a mission to minister to God's people:

> *Are they not all ministering spirits, sent forth to minister for them who shall be heirs of salvation?* (Hebrews 1:14)

From all appearances, this is the key reason for the dispatch of angels. They are ministering to the *"heirs of salvation."* Considering that humanity was made *"a little lower than the angels"* (Psalm 8:5), salvation in Christ indicates a promotion indeed.

It does not matter whether you see angels or not when they make an appearance. They are regularly in the form of an attractive human and, less frequently, as a glorious transfigured being. You may even be

Eight: Angels on Assignment

unaware of their presence. But God's eternal Word affirms that they are there.

According to **Psalm 91:12**, angels will bear you up in their hands lest you fall and dash your foot against a stone. The verse can, of course, be read both literally and metaphorically. The role of angels is to keep us from danger of all kinds, both physical and spiritual. The psalmist's choice of the word 'feet' is deliberate. Our heads may direct our thought processes, but our feet support the whole body. In the event of a real fall, the foot could also be the first part of the body to make an impact. God's angels want to keep us upright, intact and mobile. But they also want to keep us from stumbling into temptation or destroying ourselves by being caught up in evil.

For those of you who abide in God's secret place, He specially commissions the angels to keep watchful charge over you.

In every way, angels are here to deliver us from all trouble and to preserve us against enemies.

Examples of Angelic Intervention

While some may regard angels as pure fantasy, the Bible speaks of angelic existence and intervention as a powerful reality. Since angels are ministering spirits to the heirs of salvation, there are plenty of examples we can look to. They include:

- **Hagar in Genesis 16:7**: The maidservant Hagar, when pregnant with Abraham's child, fled into the wilderness to escape the wrath of her mistress Sarah. The angel found Hagar in her darkest hour, in a situation not of her own making, and ministered to her right where she was;

God's Secret Place

- **Lot in Genesis 19:16**: It was angels who spared Lot and his family from the destruction of Sodom and Gomorrah. Despite being warned of the pending danger, Lot lingered; but the angels grabbed his hand and that of his wife and two daughters and rushed them out of the city before the brimstone fell. God's mercy was upon them, and the angels were the ones who delivered it;

- **Abraham in Genesis 22:11**: God commanded Abraham to offer his son Isaac as a burnt offering. As a friend of God, Abraham learned to trust and obey, no matter what, and to do so promptly. Even though the task weighed heavily on the patriarch, he and Isaac ended up at Mount Moriah. In what must have been a most agonising moment, Abraham bound up Isaac and raised his knife in the air, ready to plunge it into his son's heart. At that very instant, the angel appeared to the patriarch and called his name. Abraham replied *Hineni* [Here I am]. The angel came with good news. He told Abraham not to harm the boy since he had proved that he feared God. Extraordinary as this event in Genesis may sound, remember that God did not ask Abraham to do anything that He wasn't willing to do Himself: He was prepared to sacrifice His Son for the sins of the world (John 3:16). Abraham trusted God because friends of God obey Him (John 15:14), even when it does not make sense. Abraham's obedience was an act of faith. But it was also tacit recognition of the doctrine of the resurrection of the dead, as affirmed in **Hebrews 11:17-19**, where we read:

> *By faith Abraham, when he was tried, offered up Isaac: and he that had received the promises offered up his only begotten son, 18. Of whom it was said, That in Isaac shall thy seed be called: 19. Accounting that God was able to raise him up, even from the dead; from whence also he received him in a figure.*

God's covenant with Abraham clearly stated that he would have innumerable descendants through the line of Isaac. God is truth and He is also a covenant-keeper. God, in His sovereignty and wisdom, wanted

Eight: Angels on Assignment

Abraham to sacrifice his son, the child of promise, while Isaac was still unmarried and childless. Abraham had faith that the promise of many children would still come through a slain Isaac via his resurrection. He trusted that even if his son died, God would restore him to life. And figuratively speaking, that's exactly what happened on the summit of Mount Moriah. Isaac's life was spared, and the lineage of Abraham continued. And angels were there to assist;

- **Jacob's wrestling match in Genesis 32:24-29**: We know that Jacob wrestled with 'a man' until the break of the day. While there is no explicit mention that he was an angel, this visitation was part of God's keeping power. Jacob had just dodged a bullet when pursued by an angry Laban, and he faced the prospect of a risky encounter with an equally furious Esau. After receiving a new name and nature (v. 28), Jacob was able to face Esau without fear. He went from being 'Jacob' to being 'Israel,' the prince of God. This, too, was another angelic assignment that changed history.

- **Israel in Exodus 14:19; 23:20-23**: In a time where there was no GPS, the angel of the Lord came to escort the children of Israel out of Egypt and put them on track to the promised land;

- **Elijah in 1 Kings 19:4-8**: This man of God had a roller coaster ride. First, there was the victorious contest against the prophets of Baal on Mount Carmel. In a short time, he went from elation to fear and despair, as Jezebel threatened to kill him. After running as far south as he could, Elijah told God that he was ready to die. In his time of fear and distress, the angel woke him up and prepared a simple meal that would sustain him for the next 40 days;

- **Jesus in Mark 1:13 and Matthew 4:1-11**: After being baptised by John, Jesus was driven by the Holy Spirit into the wilderness to be tempted for 40 days and nights. Though Satan taunted Jesus (even quoting a passage from Psalm 91) and He was amongst wild animals, we read the good news that *"the angels ministered unto him."*;

• **Peter in Acts 5:19-20; 12:7**: Twice, Peter was liberated from prison by angelic intervention;

• **Paul in the storm and before the shipwreck in Acts 27:23**: During a time of mortal danger, when Paul's ship was in a two-week storm and it was so dark that they couldn't tell day from night, something wonderful happened. One night, the angel of God appeared to Paul and encouraged him, telling him that he would make it safely to Rome so that he could appear before Caesar. Effectively, this meant that Paul would not perish at sea. And as a bonus, God spared all Paul's companions on board the ship, all 276 of them (Acts 27:37). Paul believed with his heart and saw the fulfilment of God's promise with his own eyes;

• **Book of Revelation**: More than in any other book in the Bible, angels work overtime in **Revelation**.[ii] Their activities include bringing messages to the churches; executing the seal, trumpet, and bowl judgments; and making the grand announcements that the world needs to hear. What are they? The most significant is that the temporal human kingdoms of this world are being abolished and replaced with the eternal, heavenly, divine Kingdom of God and Christ (Revelation 11:15).

The Divine Keeper

The work of angels is part of God's commitment to keep, protect, undergird, and deliver those who put their trust in Him. When Jacob fled for his life from a murderously angry Esau, God visited him at Bethel. Jacob had just tricked his father into blessing him at Esau's expense; proving that he was not in good spiritual shape (Genesis 27:11-12, 36).

Eight: Angels on Assignment

Nevertheless, God's faithfulness to the Abrahamic covenant and His merciful side were both on full display. To get Jacob's attention, He showed him a ladder between earth and heaven with the angels of God ascending and descending. Then God spoke to Jacob, solemnly promising to be with him and keep him wherever he went and whatever he did (Genesis 28:15, 20-22). Though Jacob's exile from Canaan ended up lasting twenty years, God kept His promise; He protected Jacob from Laban's abuse. The Almighty safely returned him to Canaan, married with children and possessing great substance.

While some may regard angels as pure fantasy, the Bible speaks of angelic existence and intervention as a powerful reality.

The promise of God's keeping power is not limited to one man alone. In **Psalm 34:19-20**, in a passage that has also been linked to the Messiah, God promises to deliver the righteous from all afflictions. In verse 22, we also read that *"the Lord redeemeth the soul of his servants: and none of them that trust in him shall be desolate."* In harmony with **Psalm 91**, this verse confirms that God delivers the righteous from all their troubles and keeps them intact. In addition, the Psalm 34 passage above also includes the impressive prediction that none of the Messiah's bones will be broken (v. 20). This Messianic prophecy was later fulfilled in **John 19:31-37**. While God allowed His beloved son Jesus to die for our sins, He also ensured that His body remained intact.

God's ability to protect us is based on many things: His angelic assistants; His great mercy; the power of His name (John 17:11); His marvellous peace released through prayer (Philippians 4:7); His faithfulness (2 Thessalonians 3:3); and the fact that God never slumbers nor sleeps (Psalm 121:3-4).

In his very last epistle, written from a Roman prison with no hope of release, Paul speaks in a triumphant tone: *"For I know whom I have believed, and am persuaded that he is able to keep that which I have committed unto him against that day"* (2 Timothy 1:12). Though he suffered unjust imprisonment, Paul was not ashamed because he knew the One in whom he believed. He was persuaded that the blessed object of his faith - the person of Christ - was more than able to keep what Paul committed to Him until the day of the Lord.[iii] He had completely entrusted all areas of his life to God and had absolute confidence that one day he would see the Lord face to face.

Yes, God can keep you. Believe it, receive it, and walk in it.

Watching Your Steps

The steps we take in life can make a massive difference, for better or for worse. Our steps are often determined by the decisions that we make. Let's face it: many people make wrong and foolish choices, which take them to a dead end or worse. Others do not choose at all; they just meander through life until they reach an impasse.

Considering the brevity of our natural life, it is important that we show prudence by making Godly decisions, followed up by wise and righteous steps. If we can get these two things right, we will inherit many blessings and avoid much grief.

More than once, Job speaks about how God numbers our steps (Job 14:16; 31:4). If we pursue divine wisdom, as we are exhorted to do in Proverbs, then we will find that God will direct our steps (16:9), and they will not be hindered (4:12).

Salvation and Divine Direction

Ultimately, divine direction, beautiful feet, and the blessed walk of faith are the result of receiving the gospel of eternal salvation. A good illustration of this is found in **Psalm 40:1-3**. Initially, the psalmist (David) was in the worst possible place - in the mud and clay at the bottom of a

Eight: Angels on Assignment

dark, horrible pit. The pit was so deep that there was no way, humanly speaking, that the psalmist could escape by his own devices. Even if he were as agile as a mountain goat, the walls were too high, the opening was too small, and the mud kept him glued to the bottom.

Yet help was available - heavenly help. A wonderful Saviour extended the ropes of salvation and pulled him out. Where he ended up was life-changing: he was no longer in the sinking mud but firmly on a rock. From there, God established his pathway - there was an ordained place for his feet.

In other words, God heard the psalmist's cry for help and deliverance from the deepest depths. He was brought up from the lowest and filthiest of places to the highest heights, from the messy mud to the firm foundation.

If we place our trust in God, He will order our steps: if we cooperate, He will put a 'new song' in our mouth, which is praise to God. Many will see this, receive the fear of the Lord, and put their trust in Him. From the bottom of the pit to the top of the rock, from darkness to light, from cries of despair to praise of God, our hero has travelled more than a million miles in a mere three verses and becomes a great evangelist in the process.

Since God can and will order your steps, the wisest thing you can do is to cooperate with Him. Of course, we have free will and can do as Jonah did - go west to Tarshish when God said to go east to Nineveh. In the end, the man of God would do the right thing. But look at the price he paid: three days and nights in the belly of the great fish. This ocean sojourn should have spelled death; yet God showed mercy to the wayward prophet and he was delivered (see the second chapter of the Book of Jonah).

God's Secret Place

Fall Prevention

Even when we are in the right relationship with the Almighty and are walking on the pathway He chooses, there is still the danger of missteps, tripping or stumbling. This may (or may not) be avoidable, but the promise of **Psalm 91** is that God will help keep us from falling and keep us on track. The angels will keep us in all our ways, bearing us up in their hands before we dash our feet against the stone (Psalm 91:11-12).

God is able and willing to keep us from falling. **Jude 1:24** affirms a twofold work by God in the life of the believer: His 'keeping power' and His 'perfecting power.' Despite the temptations and seductions of this world, we can remain faithful to God by virtue of His protective and upholding power. If we abide in the fear of the Lord (Proverbs 16:6) and grow in character, we can be confident that we will never stumble (2 Peter 1:10).

In addition, Jude assures us that the Lord will fine-tune, perfect, and present us faultless and flawless before God's glorious presence; and we will be full of joy. This is the promise of salvation. God's might and majesty are laid out in the wonderful doxology at the end of Jude's Epistle: *"To the only wise God our Saviour, be glory and majesty, dominion and power, both now and ever. Amen"* (Jude 1:25).

Further Illustrations of God's Oversight

There are other facets to God's promise to watch our steps. They include:

- **Enlarged steps** (Psalm 18:36): To prevent stumbling, God enlarges the steps before us.

- **Eagle's wings** (Exodus 19:4): After Pharaoh agreed to release the Hebrew people from slavery, he soon repented of his decision. Israel's steps out of Egypt needed to be swift for their oppressors were intent on stopping them from going far. God speaks of bearing His people on

Eight: Angels on Assignment

eagle's wings, which alludes to the supernatural aspect of their deliverance. The result was that He brought them to Himself.

- **God's Right hand** (Isaiah 41:10): Here, encapsulated in the powerful image of His mighty right arm, we see another wonderful example of God's promise to help those He loves. He commands us to *"fear not."* For He will impart strength to us, help us, and uphold us with His righteous right hand (see also Psalm 18:35). Of course, who is at God's right hand? Jesus Christ Himself (Luke 22:69; Acts 5:31; Romans 8:3).

- **Everlasting arms** (Deuteronomy 33:27): God promises overriding protection. He is called 'eternal' and, by His very nature, He is the perfect refuge. Not only is He God above in the heavens, but He is also God underneath you with His strong, everlasting arms. Either He will walk with you on the ordained path, or He will carry you in His arms. Whichever way, you will reach your divine destination.

- **Four-fold act** (Isaiah 46:3-4): No one looks forward to old age, with its potential infirmities and limitations. Yet we need not fear the passage of time or the whitening of our hair. From youth to old age, God promises to be present with us and, if needs be, to carry us. He does a four-fold work: as Creator, He makes us; He will pick us up (let God do the heavy lifting); He will carry us; and He will deliver us. This does not sound like a God who is cold and distant but One who is passionately interested in the welfare of His people.

These examples confirm that whether by direct intervention or by use of angels, God will guide our steps and keep us from falling. Like a good shepherd, He guards and guides His sheep. And the angels are there to help. We can draw both comfort and support from the work of these often invisible but powerful beings who labour on our behalf.

In the next chapter, however, we will confront creatures and spiritual forces that are menacing and able to inspire great fear. But drawing on the assurances of **Psalm 91**, we know that we need never be afraid. We can overcome all things.

---

[i] All reference statistics on 'angel' and 'angels' are provided courtesy of blueletterbible.org and Bible Study Version 6.10.1 from Olive Tree Bible Software.

[ii] As mentioned earlier, the word 'Angels' is mentioned twenty-two times; and 'angel' fifty-one times in Revelation.

[iii] The 'Day of the Lord' is a synonym for the last days of human rule and the transition to the Kingdom of God. It includes many key events and signs, especially the visible, bodily, and personal return of Jesus Christ to planet earth. The study of the end-times is known as *eschatology*, 'the doctrine of last things.'

CHAPTER NINE

Wild Animals Subdued

Thou shalt tread upon the lion and adder [cobra]: the young lion and the dragon [serpent] shalt thou trample under feet - **Psalm 91:13**

The Biblical Christian life is intended to be a life of victory because God gives us overcoming power. In that, we can greatly rejoice. Yet there are also implications to this: to overcome and gain victory, we have to have something to overcome. A battle is to be waged. While our key verse speaks about overcoming lions and serpents (and there are examples in Scripture of both), we can also use the same principles to prevail over enemies both human and visible and spiritual and invisible. So we need to address the threat of danger.

In our unredeemed state, we are prisoners of war at the mercy of Satan's powers. But as born-again believers, we have been liberated from the greatest of enemies: sin, sickness, the world, danger, the devil, death and hell. All these things are under Christ's feet, and His victory extends to us as well. Yet absolute and permanent victory still lies in the future.

In the meantime, as we come into God's secret place, we will learn how to tread on enemy forces should they attack us. Living on God's territory means learning from Him about perfect victory. In this chapter, we will learn more about 'how to win' from a practical viewpoint.

Treading Down the Enemy (v. 13)

Verse 13 includes a reference to a variety of menacing beasts, which were even more daunting in antiquity than they are today. After all, how many of us run into lions, adders or dragons? While it is likely that this verse was intended to apply literally to overcoming animals in real-life situations, it seems clear that these creatures were also intended to be a metaphor for every kind of danger that we face in our daily lives. So they should be understood to apply equally to human and spiritual adversaries. But for now, let's take the words of verse 13 at face value.

The psalm is telling us that we can tread on the lion, adder, young lion and 'dragon.' We are clear on the meaning of lion, young or mature. But what is the adder? And what about the dragon?

'Adder' comes from the Hebrew word *pethen*, which can mean a 'snake, venomous serpent, cobra, adder or viper.'[i]

The word 'dragon' comes from the Hebrew word *tanniyn*, which can mean several things: 'dragon' (used twenty-one times in the Bible); 'serpent' (used three times); 'whale ' (used three times); and 'sea monster' (used one time). *Tanniyn* can also imply dragon, dinosaur, sea or river monster, or great serpent.[ii] That's a big menu to choose from. What can we deduce from all this? The creature is big, formidable, dangerous, and frightening.

Yet when we are walking in the principles of **Psalm 91**, we get Elisha's double-portion of blessing (2 Kings 2:9). First, we no longer need to be afraid of these menacing adversaries. Second, we can go on the offensive and tread upon them until they are smashed to the ground.

Mankind's Dominion over God's Creatures

In one sense, this should not be surprising. The dominion of humanity over the created order is affirmed early in Scripture. We read in **Genesis 1:26** that man is made in the image of God, and he will have dominion over the fish, fowls, cattle, and everything that walks on the earth. God

Nine: Wild Animals Subdued

has this authority, and He can delegate it to whomsoever He chooses. This was *His idea*, not ours.

Then there came the fall, the introduction of sin and death, and a terrible flood. Yet the dominion aspect remained intact. After the flood, God blessed Noah by giving him specific instructions. He was commanded to replenish the earth with his own family. In **Genesis 9:2**, God also promised him that:

> *The fear of you and the dread of you shall be upon every beast of the earth and upon every bird of the heavens, upon everything that creeps on the ground and all the fish of the sea. Into your hand they are delivered.*

This sounds too good to be true: are sharks, hippos, grizzly bears, cobras and whales living in fear and dread of humans? On the surface, that would seem preposterous. But think about it - who's running this planet - the great creatures or humanity, made in the image of God?

God affirmed the ultimate dominion of humankind over the animal world. The beasts on the ground, fowls in the air, and fish in the sea all come under the stewardship that God gave to Noah and his descendants. **Psalm 8:6** also affirms that humanity has *"dominion over the works of* [God's] *hands"* - the created order - and that God has *"put all things under* [man's] *feet."* This phrase is an idiom for authority.

Ultimately, this issue of human authority culminated in the Lord Jesus Christ Himself. **Hebrews 2:8** teaches that all things are in subjection under His feet and since we are His body, all things are under our feet too. It appears, however, that some of that dominion may have been compromised due to sin and the fall of Adam. Yet in Christ, the promise of all things being under the feet was fulfilled. Christ, the second Adam, regained the paradise, purity, and dominion originally intended for the first Adam (Revelation 1:6; 5:10; Matthew 25.21).

God's Secret Place

Then, as in Hebrews, a parallel passage in **James 3:7** affirms that the animal world has been made subject to and tamed by humanity; and that Jesus, as both Son of Man and Son of God, has this authority.

We highlight this issue of dominion because it was God's original intention that the ones made in His image would rule and reign with Him. So much was forfeited through sin; but as we submit to the wisdom of **Psalm 91**, we can tread down the most ferocious of animals. It was God's will from the very beginning, backed up by His Word and power.

Hebrews 2:8 teaches that all things are in subjection under his feet, and since we are His body, all things are under our feet too.

The overcoming of ferocious animals is not poetic license. It is recorded in Scripture. Here are some examples:

- **Lions**: The word 'lion' is used one hundred and two times in the Bible, though not always literally. Phrases such as 'rescue from lions' or 'rescue from the lion's mouth' are often used as a metaphor for rescue from death (e.g. Psalm 22:21; Psalm 35:17; Psalm 58:6).[iii]

- **Samson and the lion** (Judges 14:5-8): While going down to Timnath to be with his Philistine wife, Samson encountered a young but fiery lion roaring against him. You might have thought that Samson had read **Psalm 91** because he tore the lion apart as if it were a kid goat. Please understand that Samson was strong but he was not that strong. The source of his strength was the Holy Spirit, which *"came mightily upon him"* (Judges 14:6; 16:28). After the lion's death, his carcass became a bee-hive and formed the basis of Samson's wedding riddle; the outcome resulted in a minor defeat for Samson but a great defeat for the Philistines (Judges 14:11-19). Just as Samson received power from the Spirit, so can you. Jesus promised this in **Acts 1:8**.

Nine: Wild Animals Subdued

- **David the lion slayer** (1 Samuel 17:34-37): David, son of Jesse, was a teenager when he confronted the giant Goliath of Gath. Part of the reason he confidently believed he would win the fight was because of his prior experience in the wilderness watching over his father's flocks. There, when a lion or a bear threatened a lamb from his flock, David actively went out after it and rescued it (vv. 34-35). On one such occasion, after snatching the lamb from the lion's mouth, David grabbed the lion by the beard and slew him. David, too, had **Psalm 91** protection and courage.

- **Benaiah** (1 Chronicles 11:22): Benaiah was one of David's strong, mighty men, and was also the executioner of David's son Adonijah, his nephew Joab, and Shimei (1 Kings 2). This man slew a lion in a pit while it was snowing, something that does happen in the hill country of Judah. He also killed 'two-lion like men of Moab,' which would be akin to slaying a real lion (11:22).

- **Daniel** (6:21-22): If anyone needed the refuge of **Psalm 91**, it was Daniel, the prophet from Babylon. Having been thrown into the lion's den by King Darius for the crime of praying to his God, Daniel faced great danger and his faith was put to the test. The regretful king, who reluctantly ordered the execution, had a sleepless night. When the morning came, he rushed down to the mouth of the den to see what happened. He called out to Daniel and, to his amazement, Daniel replied and explained what happened: God's angel had come to the den and shut the lions' mouths so they could not hurt him. The reason for his preservation was that he was innocent before God and had done nothing untoward to the king (v. 22). By royal decree, Daniel's accusers, who had set him up, were themselves thrown into the den and devoured, just as Haman was hanged on his own gallows for his wrongdoing (Esther 7:10).

- **Paul and the lions** (2 Timothy 4:17-18): Paul the great apostle was gutsy and courageous. He was not afraid of anything or anyone. In his

God's Secret Place

last recorded words, he was relatively upbeat though he knew his end was near. Paul commented on three things: God would deliver him *"from every evil work"*; God would preserve him safely *"unto his heavenly kingdom"*; and he was already delivered from *"the mouth of the lion."* It is debatable whether this was a literal lion or a metaphor for other frightening afflictions and persecutions which he had endured (2 Timothy 3:11).

From all these experiences, what can we glean? When trials come, the pressure increases, and natural resources prove limited, it is imperative to advance (or retreat, depending on your view) to God's secret place. Be prepared to fight the good fight of faith (1 Timothy 6:12). Draw close to Him and He will draw close to you (James 4:8).

Put on the whole armour of God (Ephesians 6:10-18). Remember the power of prayer, along with praise and worship. As high praises are in your mouth, you will wield the proverbial two-edged sword in your hand (Psalm 149:6-9). Do these things and you will have Samson, David, and Daniel-type results.

Getting our Definitions Straight: Adders and Dragons

While we have focused on overcoming lions, there are other dangerous animals listed in verse 13 that we also need to consider: the adder and the dragon. These are the words used in the King James Version. But please note that in the New King James Version, the word 'adder' is translated as 'cobra' and the word 'dragon' is translated as 'serpent.'

Adders and Cobras

But let's start with adders. As we have already seen, the Hebrew word *pethen* means cobra, adder or viper.[iv] Another name for serpent is *nahash*, also meaning snake. Though not explicitly mentioned in Genesis, the serpent encountered by Eve in the Garden of Eden was most likely not

Nine: Wild Animals Subdued

the fearful, repulsive creature that we see today. Since everything that God made in the beginning was good, that would have included the serpent too. One Bible teacher has surmised that the serpent was an attractive, alluring creature.[v] But it was certainly crafty before the Fall. Chances are that *ophidiophobia* - an abnormal fear of snakes - did not exist until after the curse was pronounced. The 'craftiness' of the serpent may have been due to its voluntary or involuntary cooperation with Satan.

After the perfect world in the Garden of Eden was overturned, God pronounced judgment on the serpent, declaring that it would be cursed more than all livestock and beasts of the field; and it would also travel on its belly and eat the dust all its days (Genesis 3:14).

Then we find in verse 15 what is believed to be the first Messianic prophecy in the Bible. Instead of cooperation, God declared that there would be a conflict between the serpent and the woman and between their descendants. In addition, man would bruise the serpent's head and the serpent would bruise his heel. These words are considered to be a reference to the crucifixion of Christ and to His victory over Satan and death following His resurrection. Bible teacher David Guzik says of this passage: "Genesis 3:15 has been called the *protoevangelium*, the first gospel. Luther said of this verse: 'This text embraces and comprehends within itself everything noble and glorious that is to be found anywhere in the Scriptures.'"[vi]

Since everything that God made in the beginning was good, that would have included the serpent too.

From Genesis 3 onwards, any reference to adders, snakes, or serpents in Scripture is profoundly negative. The tribe of Dan was likened to a serpent/adder that bites the horse's heel, causing the rider to fall backward (Genesis 49:17). The wicked are likened to poison as deadly as a serpent and to a *"deaf adder"* that stops up its ears (Psalm 58:4).

We are warned to watch out for an evil person as we would for a lurking serpent. Their tongue is just as sharp and *"poison is under their lips"* (Psalm 140:3). Proverbs warns against the use of too much wine and strong drink. When mishandled, it bites like a serpent and stings like an adder (Proverbs 23:30-31).

Dragons

Let's turn now to the topic of 'dragons,' which verse 13 tells us are meant to be as vulnerable to the **Psalm 91** believer as any other creature. We already know that the Hebrew word for dragon is *tanniyn*. The Greek New Testament word is *drakon*, a mythological monster that doubles as a metaphor for Satan himself (Revelation 12:9).[vii] But based on the NKJV translation, 'dragon' in verse **Psalm 91:13** could also be a larger serpent.

While we can debate the dragon's exact identity, it is something to be avoided but not feared - at least, not when God is your refuge and strength. What is beyond question is that the dragon, however evil and terrifying, is still able to be conquered.

Out of nineteen references to 'dragon' in Scripture, twelve are found in the **Book of Revelation** alone.[viii] Since this final book in the New Testament describes the return of the Messiah to earth and the defeat of the dragon - the ultimate of all victories - the metaphor of the dragon and its destruction in **Revelation** is a powerful one. It gives us confidence in the promises of Psalm 91.

Who then is the 'dragon'? Though much of Revelation is highly symbolic, in this instance, the symbol is thoroughly explained. **Revelation 12:9** speaks about the great dragon being cast out of heaven. He is also known as that 'old serpent' (referencing the Garden of Eden), the devil and Satan (Revelation 20:2). Thus, it can be seen that the dragon is another name for the old serpent, the devil, or Satan.

Nine: Wild Animals Subdued

This formulation is repeated in **Revelation 20:2**. In both cases, this multi-labelling of the dragon takes place when it is being demoted. The first instance is when the dragon is cast out of heaven to earth and the second is when it is bound up and cast into the bottomless pit for a thousand years.

Our Overcoming Power as Believers

The Bible is replete with references to Christ and believers having victory over the devil and demons. Through God, we will tread under those who rise up against us (Psalm 44:5); and the fear of the Lord in us will empower us to tread down the wicked (Malachi 4:2-3). Christ Himself grants believers power to tread over serpents, scorpions, and all the power of the enemy. He concludes that nothing, by any means, shall hurt us (Luke 10:19).

Those who follow and obey the Lord are vested with His authority, especially over the evil one and his minions.

As we can see, the promises to tread down the lion, adder, young lion and dragon are not unique to **Psalm 91**. Those who follow and obey the Lord are vested with His authority, especially over the evil one and his minions. The devil is like the roaring lion, that crafty old serpent, the ruby-red dragon (Revelation 12:3). Yet we who believe shall tread on Satan under our feet, courtesy of *"the God of peace"* (Romans 16:20). Jesus has disarmed all our spiritual enemies by His death on the cross. Knowing that He has *"spoiled principalities and powers"* and triumphed over them (Colossians 2:15) allows us to remain strong whatever the circumstances. He has rendered us *"more than conquerors through him that loved us"* (Romans 8:37).

Here are some faith-building promises that confirm the promise in verse 13 of **Psalm 91** that we can overcome the power of the adversary:

God's Secret Place

- **1 John 4:3-4**: *"Ye are of God, little children, and have overcome them [the spirit of antichrist]: because greater is he that is in you, than he that is in the world."*

- **Isaiah 54:17**: *"No weapon that is formed against thee shall prosper; and every tongue that shall rise against thee in judgment thou shalt condemn. This is the heritage of the servants of the LORD, and their righteousness is of me, saith the LORD."*

- **1 John 3:8**: *"He that committeth sin is of the devil; for the devil sinneth from the beginning. For this purpose the Son of God was manifested, that he might destroy the works of the devil."*

- **James 4:7**: *"Submit yourselves therefore to God. Resist the devil, and he will flee from you."*

The amazing thing about **Psalm 91** is that it offers provision and protection far beyond what we could wish for or imagine. It fills our hearts with hope, drives out our fears, and grants supernatural strength where faintheartedness might otherwise dominate. For this reason, we must hold the words of Psalm 91 in our hearts every day, no matter how difficult our situation may be.

As we continue and conclude, the best is yet to come.

---

[i] "H6620 - pethen - Strong's Hebrew Lexicon (NASB)." Blue Letter Bible. Accessed 1 Dec, 2020. https://www.blueletterbible.org//lang/lexicon/lexicon.cfm?Strongs=H6620&t=NASB.

"H8577 - tanniyn - Strong's Hebrew Lexicon (KJV)." Blue Letter Bible. Accessed 1 Dec, 2020. https://www.blueletterbible.org//lang/lexicon/lexicon.cfm?Strongs=H8577&t=KJV.

Nine: Wild Animals Subdued

---

iii "KJV Search Results for "lion"." Blue Letter Bible. Accessed 6 Aug, 2022. https://www.blueletterbible.org//search/search.cfm?Criteria=lion&t=KJV#s=s_primary_0_1.

iv See the chapter *No-Fear Zone*.

v Nancy deMoss Wolgemuth, 'Deception and Discernment Teaching Series, *Revive Our Hearts Ministries, https://www.reviveourhearts.com/.*

vi Guzik, D. "Study Guide for Genesis 3 by David Guzik." Blue Letter Bible. Last Modified 21 Feb, 2017. https://www.blueletterbible.org/Comm/guzik_david/StudyGuide2017-Gen/Gen-3.cfm.

vii Because of Revelation 12:9, we have the following equation:

Dragon = Old Serpent = Devil = Satan.

"KJV Search Results for "dragon"." Blue Letter Bible. Accessed 6 Aug, 2022. https://www.blueletterbible.org//search/search.cfm?Criteria=dragon&t=KJV#s=s_primary_0_1.

CHAPTER TEN

Deliverance and Promotion

Because he hath set his love upon me, therefore will I deliver him: I will set him on high, because he hath known my name.15 He shall call upon me, and I will answer him: I will be with him in trouble; I will deliver him, and honour him. 16 With long life will I satisfy him, and shew him my salvation **- Psalm 91:14-16**.

We are coming to the final stretch of **Psalm 91**, namely the last three verses. Contained within verses 14-16 are some extraordinary promises: deliverance from trouble, promotion on high, and favour with God through answered prayer. Even more important is the pledge by God to be with those who love Him, when they are in trouble, and not to leave them there. They will be completely delivered by God, emerge from the strife and, as a bonus, receive vindication and honour. Then God promises to give them long life and to reveal His salvation to them.

Here in this chapter, we will focus on verse 14 and the promises of deliverance and promotion. What wonderful and priceless things these promises are. But is there anything we need to do to receive them? The answer is that we are called to *"set [our] love upon [God]."*

Setting our Love upon God (v. 14)

Since God is love (1 John 4:8), loving God means that we are only returning to Him that which He lavishes on us. It was love that caused God to create us, redeem us, and give us a city with foundations and a kingdom that never ends.

God's Secret Place

For more guidance on how to love God, which - by extension - releases all the above benefits, let's hear about the subject from the very mouth of Jesus. Responding to a question about what is the most important commandment of all, He said:

> *The first of all the commandments is, Hear, O Israel; The Lord our God is one Lord: 30 And thou shalt love the Lord thy God with all thy heart, and with all thy soul, and with all thy mind, and with all thy strength: this is the first commandment.* (Mark 12:29-30)

Jesus quotes this passage - known by the Jewish people as *The Shema* ('listen' or 'hear') - comes straight out of the law in **Deuteronomy 6:4-5**. For all practical purposes, the *Shema* is Israel's national creed distilled into two simple commands; and it is recited daily by pious Jews. Jesus was a Torah-observant Jew and by referencing the *Shema* (Mark 12:29), He was asserting His Jewish credentials.

Loving God is not just a theoretical injunction or a poetic abstraction; it is a lifestyle choice. We are to love God with all our being, including all our heart, all our soul, all our mind, and all our strength. Every part of our being is covered: body, mind, soul and spirit. Jesus adds that loving God is the first commandment. Add to this the directive to love your neighbour as yourself (Mark 12:31), and then all the law and the prophets have been encapsulated in these two commandments (Matthew 22:37-40).

Demonstrating our Love for God

If you want examples of loving God the way He wants to be loved and the showers of blessing which pour down, as a result, look no further than the **Book of Psalms**. Even without mentioning the word 'love,' the psalmists make it clear that getting into God's presence is their highest priority. Just as some people love the pub, the sporting arena, the television or some other form of entertainment including their

Ten: Deliverance and Promotion

smartphones, the one who loves God can't wait to come to the Throne of Grace. The sons of Korah[i] longed, even fainted, just to be in God's courts, which were not even in the inner sanctum of the Temple. Their heart and flesh cried out for God (Psalm 84:2), and they loved Him with all their strength to the point of exhaustion. Just as the hart pants for water in a parched place, so the souls of these sons of Korah panted after the living God (Psalm 42:1).

The psalmist Asaph confessed that there was nothing on earth he desired more than God (Psalm 73:25); and if he looked in heaven, there was no one else but God. Of course, heaven also contains angels, heavenly hosts, and the spirits of just men made perfect - the general assembly and church of the firstborn who are written in heaven (Hebrews 12:23). But what he was saying was that, above all, he wanted to draw close to God and be in His presence.

On earth, love for God is demonstrated by making Him the sole (and soul) focus of our life. By saying that there is no one else in heaven but God, Asaph affirms His singularity and the fact that He is the only God. The psalmists' desire for God outweighs everything else, including the love of people and other physical things.

The following verses reflect the same need for wholehearted devotion to God, but they also highlight God's goodness in response:

- **Psalm 31:23**: Love the Lord - he preserves the faithful.

- **Psalm 97:10**: You who love the Lord, hate evil. He will preserve and deliver the saints who love Him.

- **Psalm 116:1**: The psalmist loves God because He answers prayer.

- **Psalm 145:20**: Again, as **Psalm 91** promises, the Lord preserves them that love Him, but will destroy the wicked.

God's Secret Place

- **1 John 4:19**: Straight and simple: we can love God because He first loved us.

While we can express our love for God in words, it is real actions that ultimately count. As the adage goes, 'Talk is cheap.' We demonstrate the love of God in a variety of ways but to keep it simple, those who love God walk with God.

Enoch

We find a famous example of this in the brief account of Enoch in **Genesis 5:22-24**. He was the father of Methuselah, the oldest man in the Bible at 969 years, and he was also the father of other sons and daughters. His entire natural life spanned 365 years. There is nothing remarkable about any of this except perhaps his age. What is remarkable is that twice in two verses, Enoch is commended for the same thing - that he *"walked with God."*

When the Bible says something once, that is sufficient. When it says something twice, take extra notice. Enoch walked with God because he loved God. Then something amazing occurred. He completely disappeared from the planet without a trace. Why did this happen? It's simple. God took Enoch so that he would not experience death (Hebrews 11:5); and He did this in recognition of Enoch's love for Him and his walk with Him. Enoch's unexpected disappearance (known as 'translation') demonstrated that the Almighty's feelings for Enoch were mutual.

Noah

Noah loved God because he also walked with Him. In **Genesis 6:9**, he is described as a just and perfect man, a special commendation considering how perverse his generation was. They were so bad that God would

Ten: Deliverance and Promotion

wipe them out with a flood. But because Noah loved and walked with the Lord, then in true **Psalm 91** fashion, God pledged to deliver him. And deliver him He did, by directing the construction of the ark which preserved Noah's family, land animals, and fowls of the air.

Levi

If we turn to **Malachi 2:5-6**, we learn that Levi was a righteous priest, who feared the Lord and *"was afraid before [His]name."* His mouth was clean because *"[t]he law of truth was in his mouth,"* and iniquity could not be found there. He was an upholder of God's Word. All of this was made possible because *"he walked with [God] in peace and equity."* And as a bonus, he turned many away from their iniquities to do likewise.

New Testament Examples

Of course, loving God and walking with Him are also prized in the New Testament. God remembers the labours of love that we perform in His name as we minister to the saints (Hebrews 6:10). Yet our actions must be righteous. In **Revelation 3:1-6**, the church at Sardis promoted itself as an 'alive/action-orientated church' and convinced many of the same. However, the One whose opinion counted the most - Christ - thought otherwise. To this church, He made a stark declaration that they were *"dead."*

Despite this, there was recognition that even in dead Sardis, a few saints did not defile their garments and were worthy. These will walk before Christ clothed in righteous white.

Knowing God

It is a fundamental yet profound truth that the key to loving God is to know God. It is not enough merely to know about Him; or to have cerebral cognisance of, or exercise mental assent to, Him. The key is to know God personally. This is such a core issue that it serves as the very definition of eternal life. Jesus, in His masterful intercessory prayer for His present and future disciples, says in **John 17:3**: *"[T]his is life eternal, that they might know thee the only true God, and Jesus Christ, whom thou hast sent."*

Yes, eternal life is knowing God. Think about this for a moment, and it makes good sense. After all, the Lord fills heaven and earth, and there is no searching of His understanding (Isaiah 40:28). Yet He wants you to know Him. How long does it take to 'know' or 'master' God? It should be obvious that it takes an eternity. It takes an equal amount of time to thank Jesus Christ for being a great Saviour and for giving us a great salvation.

On earth, love for God is demonstrated by making Him the sole (and soul) focus of your life.

Like any relationship, it takes time to know the other party. A lack of personal, spiritual devotions or perfunctory ones that merely offer God the crumbs of our day will not suffice. The most important time of your day is your appointment with God. It need not be long, but it should always be qualitative. And, of course, the time spent may vary. Yet the knowledge of God brings something everyone craves: promotion, recognition, and blessing.

A Deeper Understanding of the Character of God

If you walk with God, you will discover that He is not distant, austere, or unkind. On the contrary, when you understand and know Him, you can glory in the fact that God practises and delights in lovingkindness, judgment, and righteousness on earth (Jeremiah 9:24). Just as the former (or early) and the latter (or late) rains in the Bible are essential for planting the seed and then reaping the harvest, so too those who press

Ten: Deliverance and Promotion

on to know God will be visited with refreshing, life-giving rains, both spiritually and physically (Hosea 6:3).

The notion of 'knowing Christ' is wonderful indeed. Yet this same Son of David, Son of God, Messiah, Saviour and King is also the One who suffered unspeakably for our sins and our sake. Since we are to become agents of change in the world, we need to know the One who conquered sin; destroyed the work of the devil; trampled over sickness; triumphed over principalities and powers; and lives forevermore.

Understanding Christ was such a passion for the apostle Paul that he wanted to know everything about the person of Christ, including *"the power of his resurrection, and the fellowship of his sufferings, being made conformable unto his death"* (Philippians 3:8-10).

If you find this daunting, remember that you can't know spiritual resurrection power until your carnal self is put to death on the cross. Paul's transformation from persecutor of early Christians to an ardent follower of Jesus did bring brokenness; but out of the brokenness came a great spiritual anointing, just as the breaking of the alabaster box released the precious ointment in the house of Simon the leper (Mark 14:3-9). Paul's zealous pursuit of the knowledge of Christ plus his single-minded gospel focus and personal tenacity are what caused him to be a world changer. Without question, he is one of the most influential people in history.

To know Christ includes understanding, among other things, that:

1. His yoke is easy and His burden light (Matthew 11:30);

2. He has overcome the world (John 16:33);

3. He is meek and lowly of heart (Matthew 11:29);

4. He is Alpha and Omega, the beginning and the end, the first and the last (Revelation 22:13);

5. He is high above all principalities, power, might, dominion and every name that is named (Ephesians 1:21);

6. He is the king of glory (Psalm 24:8,10);

7. He is ever gentle: a bruised reed He will not break and a smoking flax He will not quench (Isaiah 42:3; Matthew 12:20);

8. All authority is given to Him in heaven and on earth (Matthew 28:18).

Benefits of Knowing God

Knowing Christ's truth has the wonderful power of setting you free (John 8:31,32) from the slavery stain, and stench of sin. It gives you discernment about true versus false doctrine. And make no mistake about it: sound doctrine helps build a solid walk with God; false doctrine can send you on the wrong path. Right doctrine promotes wisdom, favour, grace and peace in the believer, while false doctrine will make you stumble and fall.

Christ's truth is also a mark of discipleship. Paul's greeting to the Colossian church is a wonderful benediction to all. His prayer was that *"[they] might walk worthy of the Lord unto all pleasing, being fruitful in every good work, and increasing in the knowledge of God"* (Colossians 1:10). To grow in the knowledge of God is to position yourself for promotion.

Knowing the truth is simple. Yet it takes time and commitment to a lifestyle of prayer; study of the Scriptures; quality Christian fellowship; praise; worship and thanksgiving; and obedience. All these will lead you to a place of ascending the mountain of the Lord. And the view from the

Ten: Deliverance and Promotion

top is out of this world. But as Peter acknowledges, you will also want to give God the glory.

> *But grow in grace, and in the knowledge of our Lord and Saviour Jesus Christ. To him be glory both now and for ever. Amen.* (2 Peter 3:18)

While we acknowledge and endorse a lifestyle of knowing God, there is a particular aspect of God - His Name - which is the key to all other parts of the knowledge. We will learn more about this in the next section.

God's Name Saves, Protects, and Promotes

As we learned in chapter 1, God's Name is not just a key that unlocks the door to the divine refuge - His Name is the refuge (Proverbs 18:10). So let's go deeper into this vital subject. All along, we have seen that God promises to deliver those who put their trust in Him, and **Psalm 91** confirms this truth. Deliverance from fear, disease, danger and the weapons of the enemy is a priceless gift. Yet as we see here in verse 14, those who love and walk with God will not just be delivered - they will be promoted. For the Lord says that He will set them on high for knowing his name.

And make no mistake about it. Sound doctrine helps build a solid walk with God; false doctrine can send you on the wrong path.

God's name is the key to God Himself. It is the source of authority and salvation. So what should we do regarding His name? As we already know, we do have a Name - a divine pronounceable Name - that unlocks all of heaven's manifold blessings.[ii]

Jesus Christ - who was humbled to the point of death on the cross, raised to life, ascended to heaven, and is seated at the right hand of God - has the Name which is above all names (Philippians 2:9). One day, every other power, potentate, president, prince, prime minister, and every source of authority, seen and unseen, will bow the knee to this Name (v. 10).

Salvation lies in the Name of Jesus (Yeshua)

In the light of this, it is not surprising, then, that we learn in **Acts 4:12** that calling on the name of Jesus is the only means of salvation:

> *Neither is there salvation in any other: for there is none other name under heaven given among men, whereby we must be saved.*

That's right - salvation is found in the name of Jesus. And this is reflected in the name which He bears. The angel of the Lord informed Joseph in a dream that the child in Mary's womb would be named Yeshua (Jesus) for He would save His people from their sins (**Matthew 1:21**). Yeshua is the diminutive of *Yehoshua,* the Hebrew name for Joshua. It is translated as 'Yahweh is salvation.'[iii] You can't get more precise than that. By believing in His Name, you will have the gift of (eternal) life (John 20:31).

The prophet Isaiah gives us the amplified version of Yeshua's name. In **Isaiah 9:6**, he proclaims:

> *For unto us a child is born, unto us a son is given: and the government shall be upon his shoulder: and his name shall be called Wonderful, Counsellor, The mighty God, The everlasting Father, The Prince of Peace.*

This passage tells us that the child and son would be born in, and for Israel. What's the name of this Son? It is Wonderful, Counsellor, the mighty God, the everlasting Father, the Prince of Peace. We are also told that the government will be on His shoulders. And of the growth of His kingdom and peace, there will be no end once He inherits the throne of David (Isaiah 9:7). He is the *"KING OF KINGS, AND LORD OF LORDS"* - **Revelation 19:16**.

Ten: Deliverance and Promotion

Although Yeshua (Jesus) was born a man, He was simultaneously called the *"mighty God"* (Isaiah 9:6). And as we have already learned, Jesus had to be God to save us and man to die for us.[iv] But the key to salvation is calling on the Name of Yeshua (Saviour).

According to Scripture, the glorious gospel of Christ is that He died for our sins, was buried, and rose from the dead on the third day (1 Corinthians 15:3-5). But salvation must be accompanied by repentance and faith. In **Luke 24:47**, Jesus told his disciples that *"repentance and remission of sins should be preached in His Name to all nations,"* starting in Jerusalem.

Once you know and walk with Yeshua/Jesus, you have unparalleled power and authority. He will be in your midst when two or three are gathered together in His Name (Matthew 18:20). We have power in prayer (John 14:13), and we can perform signs and wonders in His name (Mark 16:17). In His matchless Name, there is healing and wholeness (Acts 3:16).

What a wonderful, mighty, glorious Name Jesus has. By knowing it, you will be saved, delivered, and set on high.

Promotion on High - Old Testament (Hebrew Scriptures)

When we first began to learn about **Psalm 91**, we may have been content simply to have God's presence and protection in our lives. Just these two things alone are priceless. However, just as the psalmist in **Psalm 23:5** has an overflowing cup, so too can those of us who dwell in the secret place and are under His Name receive a double, triple or quadruple portion of blessing that is beyond measure. We see that knowing God's Name promotes, elevates, and puts us in a position of authority that we could only begin to imagine.

Instead of being in valley bottoms, vulnerable and at the mercy of the elements and wild animals, God causes us to 'dwell on high.' This is the top of the mountain among the rocks. It may be remote, but the bread and water are bountifully provided (Isaiah 33:16).

Prayer and Fasting

Lofty dwelling in God's high places can be obtained by two of life's lowliest activities - fasting and prayer. To deny yourself food temporarily in order to seek God's face is a supreme act of humility and a pathway to power. It sends a message to the Almighty that will get His attention. It tells God that you need something from Him and that you are willing to afflict yourself to achieve that end. When people fast, God will stop and take notice. Even Jesus acknowledged that God will reward us for fasting, provided that it is not done for show but is performed 'in secret' or privately (Matthew 6:16).

Revivals, visitations, and outpourings of the Spirit are often accompanied by this spiritual discipline. It is highly recommended. However, if you have any doubts about your fitness to fast, please consult a physician first before doing so (pregnancy, diabetes, and treatment for illness are good reasons not to fast).

The definitive chapter on fasting is **Isaiah 58**. In verse 14, a host of benefits are promised. Those who partake of God's chosen fast will be joyful as they rejoice in God. They will ride on the high places of the earth. Jacob's fruitful heritage will be their great feast. All of this is guaranteed because the mouth of the Lord has spoken it. God speaks the truth and keeps His word.

Obedience and Promotion are Linked

The Hebrew prophets spoke about God's promotion on high. One of the classic passages is **Habakkuk 3:17-19**. If you obey God by rejoicing in the

Ten: Deliverance and Promotion

Lord, no matter what the circumstances may be, you will be catapulted from the bottom of the dark, narrow valley to the broad horizons visible from the mountain top. You need not - and should not - deny the reality of your circumstances, which deception and delusion may cause you to do. Instead, acknowledge the situation, and then fasten your focus on God. As you do this, God will give you the feet of a deer (hind's feet) so you can go from mountaintop to mountaintop.

Daniel goes further by promising that those who are wise in a Godly way and turn many to righteousness will shine like bright stars forever and ever (Daniel 12:3).

Being Promoted on High - New Testament (New Covenant[v])

Being *"set on high"* is a great reward from God. It is not merely an Old Testament experience, but is powerfully affirmed in the New Testament too. While the phraseology used is not always about altitude, we can still clearly see the language of promotion. In the parable of the talents in **Luke 19:17**, for example, the servant took his master's single pound/mina/talent and it became ten pounds. He was commended by the master for being a *"good servant"* and his reward was a promotion. Instead of being a steward over ten pounds, he was to have authority over ten cities. Why ten cities? The divine gauge is that faithfulness in the little things means faithfulness in the bigger things too. This servant was appointed and promoted as a leader over many.

In **1 Corinthians 6:2**, Paul highlights an intriguing promise to the faithful saints. They will be authorised, empowered, and promoted to judge the world. Since this is our promised destiny, we should have the maturity and integrity to judge even the smallest matters involving other Christians.[vi]

Another perspective on being *"seated on high"* can be found in **Ephesians 2:6**, which tells us that God has *"raised us up together, and made us sit*

God's Secret Place

together in heavenly places in Christ Jesus." But before we can be promoted to the *"heavenly places,"* we first have to die to sin and self (Romans 6:6) and be raised up *"in newness of life"* (vv. 4-5). While the vantage point is priceless, there is more concentrated spiritual activity up in the high places than down here on earth.

Spiritual Warfare and Promotion

Paul warns us in **Ephesians 6:10-20** that the Christian life in a fallen world involves a battle. The reason for this, he explains, is the existence and reality of an invisible, spiritual world, which is far more formidable than any earthly realm (v. 12). The darkness knows it is fighting a losing battle, but it persists anyway.

That's why we are told to *"be strong in the Lord, and in the power of his might"* (v. 10). And we are exhorted to put on *"the whole armour of God"* so that we can *"stand against the wiles of the devil"* (Ephesians 6:11).

As believers, we have access to the six parts of God's armour (vv. 14-17). These include:

1. The belt of truth around our waist;
2. The breastplate of righteousness on our chest;
3. The gospel of peace on our feet;
4. The shield of faith which will extinguish the fiery darts of the wicked one;
5. The helmet of salvation which protects our head and mind;
6. The sword of the Spirit, which is God's Word.

Finally, we are to pray all kinds of prayers *"in the Spirit"* and watch out in *"perseverance and supplication for all saints"* (v. 18). Do these things and you will keep standing in the evil day (v. 13), even though others may fall. Doesn't it have the ring of **Psalm 91:7**? Our ability to abide in God's

Ten: Deliverance and Promotion

secret place does hinge on *"fighting the good fight of faith"* (1 Timothy 6:12).

Promotion on High and the Book of Revelation

The last glorious book of Scripture, **Revelation**, also offers us insight into what God means by promotion. In **Chapter 4:1**, the apostle John was invited to come up higher - apparently to heaven - so God could show him future events about End Times. You may recall that **Revelation** is about the unveiling of Jesus Christ, both today and in the future, and it also outlines upcoming prophetic events (1:1). What John saw in **Revelation** has left the Church breathless for the last 2,000 years.

One extraordinary promise about promotion was given by Christ in **Revelation 2-3** as part of the letters that He gave the Apostle John for the seven churches of Asia (Minor). Every church was encouraged to be an overcomer, and great rewards were promised to those who were.

It appears that the Lord saved the best for last. In the letter to the Laodiceans (Revelation 3:14-22), He did not commend them for anything, as He did with the other churches. Instead, he delivered a blistering rebuke because of their lukewarmness. But Christ did assure Laodicea that His rebuke was based on a deep love for the church, noting that *"[a]s many as I love, I rebuke and chasten: be zealous therefore, and repent"* (v. 19).

The Laodiceans believed that they lacked for nothing, but Christ could see that they were spiritually bereft and desperately in need of what only He could offer them (vv. 17-18). Yet surprisingly, despite this, the least worthy church still received the greatest promise of all. If they could overcome their spiritual lukewarmness, acknowledge their spiritual wretchedness, and turn away from their sins, they would sit with Christ on His throne (v. 21).

God's Secret Place

We know that Christ is seated at the right hand of God. If being seated with Christ is on offer, then we need to redefine 'promotion.' The prize of sitting next to Christ on His throne was highly coveted. The sons of Zebedee made such a request of Jesus (Mark 10:37), but He did not give His assent. But here in Revelation, we read that the Lord was freely offering this place to a lukewarm church, provided they learned to overcome by heeding His voice (v.20). This is called amazing grace.

We also learn in **Revelation 11:10** that a similar invitation to *"come up"* was given to the two brave witnesses who *"tormented"* the world with their power-based, prophetic ministry. The beast (Satan) rose up from the bottomless pit and killed them (v. 7). But after three and a half days, they rose to their feet again because God's *"spirit of life entered into them"* (v. 11). Needless to say, the whole world watched in awe at these things. Then these witnesses were invited to go up to heaven (v. 12); and after their ascension, a great earthquake came within the hour (v. 13).

Our ability to abide in God's secret place does hinge on 'fighting the good fight of faith' (1 Timothy 6:12).

While Laodicea, John, and the two witnesses were offered balcony seats to future world events, what about the rest of us who believe? What lies in store for us? We also find the answer in Revelation.

When Christ takes the scroll and prepares to break the seven seals, which are the 'seal judgment,' the four creatures and twenty-four elders fall down to worship Him who sits on The Throne. He is the One who was slain and redeemed us to God by His shed blood (Revelation 5:9). This grace, forgiveness, and cleansing - the great gift of salvation – continue for us because God has made us *"kings and priests"* (Revelation 1:6; 5:10). Although we are promoted by heaven, we will reign on the earth as kings and priests. These two offices are invested with divine power and authority. So our promotion is great indeed.

Ten: Deliverance and Promotion

In the next chapter, we will see God's authority activated in the throne room of grace (Hebrews 4:16) as we experience the power of answered prayer.

---

[i] Sons of Korah are the descendants who did not participate in Korah's failed rebellion (Numbers 16) against Moses and Aaron. They were prominent in the Levitical service of the house of God.

[ii] For further coverage of this, review Chapter One: *The God of Psalm 91*.

[iii] Joshua or Yehoshua means 'God' or 'Jehovah' is salvation. "H3091 - yᵉhôšûaʿ - Strong's Hebrew Lexicon (kjv)." Blue Letter Bible. Accessed 20 Aug, 2022. https://www.blueletterbible.org/lexicon/h3091/kjv/wlc/0-1/.

[iv] See Chapter One: *The God of Psalm 91*.

[v] 'New Testament' and 'New Covenant' are synonymous. As spoken of in Jeremiah 31:31-34, the New Covenant was first made with Israel and Judah, where God promised: His law would be written on their hearts; they would know God personally; and their sins would be forgiven and forgotten. The shed blood of Christ ratified this covenant for all believers, Jew and Gentile (Luke 22:20; 1 Corinthians 11:25).

[vi] As an aside, since we will be judging angels, we should solve issues within the church without outside legal action. Taking a brother and/or sister in Christ to the law courts is strongly discouraged.

CHAPTER ELEVEN

God's Presence, Answered Prayer, and Enlargement

He shall call upon me, and I will answer him: I will be with him in trouble; I will deliver him, and honour him - **Psalm 91:15**.

As we approach the end of Psalm 91, the adage holds true that God has saved the best for last. The time of distress, the pressing into God's presence, and the laying hold of His promises in the Psalm are now starting to pay rich dividends. God's best is worth the wait.

Answered Prayer (v. 15)

The Bible-based, Spirit-filled Christian life is a life of joy. Some of the joy comes organically and supernaturally as the fruit of the Spirit (**Galatians 5:22**), while other aspects of joy are enhanced by circumstances. Yet one of the greatest joys imaginable is that of answered prayer. As **John 16:24**: promises, *"Hitherto have ye asked nothing in my name: ask, and ye shall receive, that your joy may be full."* Similarly, **Proverbs 13:12** tells us that *"[h]ope deferred maketh the heart sick: but when the desire cometh, it is a tree of life."*

Prayer is essential, even mandatory for believers. It has been said that prayer for the spiritual life is like air to the lungs. Prayerfulness leads to empowerment, while failure to pray renders us *"weak, and ... like any other man"* (Judges 16:17). It would be terrifying to be in a situation where God intentionally declines to answer prayer, as was the case with

God's Secret Place

a desperate Saul the day before his defeat and death at Mount Gilboa (1 Samuel 28:20).

God promises to answer prayer. The following scriptures give us that assurance:

- **Isaiah 58:9** (for those who fast): *"Then you shall call, and the Lord will answer; you shall cry, and he will say, 'Here I am.' If you take away the yoke from your midst, the pointing of the finger, and speaking wickedness."*

- **Isaiah 65:24**: *"Before they call I will answer; while they are yet speaking I will hear."*

- **Jeremiah 33:3**: *"Call to me and I will answer you, and will tell you great and hidden things that you have not known."*

- **Zechariah 13:9**: *"And I will put this third into the fire, and refine them as one refines silver, and test them as gold is tested. They will call upon my name, and I will answer them. I will say, 'They are my people;' and they will say, 'The Lord is my God.'"*

- **Luke 11:9** (persistence in prayer): *"And I say unto you, Ask, and it shall be given you; seek, and ye shall find; knock, and it shall be opened unto you."*

- **John 15:7** (key to prayer): *"If ye abide in me, and my words abide in you, ye shall ask what ye will, and it shall be done unto you."*

- **1 John 3:22** (obedience and God-pleasing behaviour): *"And whatsoever we ask, we receive of him, because we keep his commandments, and do those things that are pleasing in his sight."*

We can see in these passages all kinds of wonderful principles needed to receive answers in prayer. But let's return to **Psalm 91** and see for ourselves what its specific plan entails. In verse 14, we learned that love

Eleven: God's Presence, Answered Prayer, and Enlargement

of God, knowing God and, specifically, the power and authority of His Name will set us on high. When we are lifted up, our proximity to God - the source of answered prayer - and His proximity to us increase. While God can hear your cry from the valley bottom, imagine how much quicker and more effective His response can be from the mountain top.

God's Presence in Trouble (v. 15)

The promise of answers applies to all prayers, yet it is particularly relevant in times of trouble. Sometimes, we are in a stew of our own making, but there are also times when we are facing problems precisely because we are doing the right thing. The psalm does not tell us that God will always keep us from trouble; it says that He will be with us **in** trouble **and** deliver us and honour us. This is an important distinction.

Trust is the Key

God is present everywhere (omnipresent). Even without **Psalm 91**, the Scripture is adamant that God is with the righteous. The promise is that He will never leave any who trust in Him (Hebrews 13:5; John 14:16-17); indeed, He is with us to the end of the world (Matthew 28:20).

So too in **Deuteronomy 31:6**, just before all Israel was about to cross the Jordan into their new home Canaan, Moses encouraged them with these words:

Be strong and of a good courage, fear not, nor be afraid of them: for the Lord thy God, he it is that doth go with thee; he will not fail thee, nor forsake thee."

Of course, as we have already seen, there are times when God does considerably more than just be with His people in trouble. The Bible is full of stories of protection and deliverance. Consider Daniel, who had the audacity to pray to God at his window after a blanket prohibition on prayer had been issued by the King. For his righteous stance, he was cast into the lion's den (Daniel 6:13 -22). God was with Daniel in the den just as He was with Daniel's three friends in the fiery furnace (Daniel 3:25-28). In these cases, they were all supernaturally delivered.

As believers, we should continue to trust God for the same supernatural intervention, even if we do not see immediate or miraculous results. Christian maturity is contingent on our taking God at His word and walking by faith (2 Corinthians 5:7), not by sight, feelings, or perception.

Unfortunately, it is very common, especially in a postmodern, post-rational, 'post-truth' world, to view things from the vantage point of feelings. The mantra is that 'perception is reality.' In a way, there is truth to this. Take two people sitting in the same room near each other. One person says, 'I'm cold.' The second person says, 'I'm hot.' Which one is right? Technically, they both are. In the personal, thermostatic department, we are wired differently.

However, this philosophy is often extended to issues like truth and theology, and everything is said to be relative. You have your truth, I have mine, and both are equally valid. Yet if there's a universal truth - and the Biblical Christian affirms this is so - then clinging to feelings and the view that 'perception is reality' is dangerous.

Why is this? The answer is that because God is real and His Word is truth, then to 'feel' otherwise is akin to calling God a liar. And to say that God is a liar is the greatest lie of all.

The feeling-perception person might say, 'I don't feel the love of God. I don't feel God cares. God is not near.' But as believers, we need to reject this 'feelings-based reality' and choose to rely on what God's Enduring Word says. Instead of viewing the world through the postmodern prism of perception, try meditating on what Almighty God has promised:

Eleven: God's Presence, Answered Prayer, and Enlargement

- **Hebrews 13:5**: *"For he hath said, I will never leave thee, nor forsake thee."*

- **Matthew 28:20**: *"[A]nd, lo, I am with you always, even unto the end of the world. Amen."*

- **Isaiah 41:10**: *"Fear thou not; for I am with thee: be not dismayed; for I am thy God; I will strengthen thee; yea, I will help thee; yea, I will uphold thee with the right hand of my righteousness."*

- **Joshua 1:5**: *"There shall not any man be able to stand before thee all the days of thy life: as I was with Moses, so I will be with thee: I will not fail thee, nor forsake thee."*

In **Deuteronomy 4:31**, God also tells us that:

[T]he Lord thy God is a merciful God; ... he will not forsake thee, neither destroy thee, nor forget the covenant of thy fathers which he sware unto them.

From this, we learn that God is a merciful, covenant-making, covenant-keeping God. His promises are iron-clad. God will not forsake you nor destroy you. The basis of this great anchor-of-the-soul hope is the covenant that He made with Abraham in Genesis 12, 15, and 17. In the eyes of God, a covenant is a covenant, a deal is a deal.

Both Old and New Testament Promises Apply Equally to Jew and Gentile

Yet despite all these promises about God's protection, you may say that it is all 'Old Testament stuff,' which applies only to Israel. Think again. Everyone who is redeemed by their faith in Jesus - both Jew and Gentile – is a beneficiary of the New Covenant, which was originally made with the house of Israel and Judah (Jeremiah 31:31-34; Galatians 3:26-28).

God's Secret Place

But **Galatians 3:29** tells us that as believers, we are also beneficiaries of the promises God made to Israel. **Verse 29** is clear that if you belong to Christ, then you are the [spiritual] seed of Abraham, which makes you an heir *"according to the [covenant] promise."* The promise here is surely the covenantal promise of **Jeremiah 31:31-34**.

This means that you can lay claim to all of God's protective guarantees. And the testimony of Scripture is overwhelming: God promises that He will not forget, fail, forsake, nor destroy His people. On the contrary, He will remember, show mercy to, bear, carry, deliver, come to, and love them to the very end. So never doubt for a moment that God cares for you. His Word promises it, and His actions prove it.

Christian maturity is contingent on our taking God at His word and walking by faith ... not by sight, feelings or perception.

God's love is beautifully depicted in the famous poem called *Footprints in the Sand*.[i] A Christian looks over her life of faith and sees two sets of footprints in the sand: hers and God's. Yet during the most trying times of life, there is only one set of footprints. The immediate conclusion is that God has forsaken her and that she was on her own. Not so. The one set of footprints was not the believer's, but God's. He carried her during the hard times. And He will carry you too.

Trouble's Silver Lining

As we have already seen, trouble is part of being in a fallen world. When the Lord returns, this issue will be fixed once and for all, but what do we do in the meantime? It may not feel like it at the time, but trouble in the walk of faith is always a blessing in disguise. The flesh may be tempted to say, 'Keep the blessing and remove the trouble.' But many blessings call first for personal hardship or sacrifice. For example, qualifying for a university degree usually requires intensive study and successful

Eleven: God's Presence, Answered Prayer, and Enlargement

completion of final exams. And having a baby involves pregnancy and painful delivery.

No matter how difficult the situation, we know that God will take the trouble and work it for our good (Romans 8:28).

A Closer Relationship with God

One benefit is that trouble may draw us closer to God and motivate us to discover what is pleasing to Him. As **Psalm 119:67** reminds us, *"Before I was afflicted I went astray: but now have I kept thy word."*

Affliction and trouble have an amazing ability to propel us into the presence of God, where mercy and grace await us (Hebrews 4:16). Like an alarm clock or sounding of the trumpet, trials help get our attention. They can wake up the sleepers, prioritise the distracted, and cause the unfocused to walk a single path.

An offshoot of this is a greater anointing. Living a victorious, empowered Christian life requires the anointing and empowerment of the Holy Spirit. This is such a priceless gift that it can never be purchased with all the money in the world. So God gives it to us for free (John 14:16-17).

Yet like so many wonderful things, we have to position ourselves to receive it. According to Jesus, the anointed/Spirit-filled life comes by thirsting, coming to the Lord, and drinking the rivers of living water (John 7:37-39). It's not a matter of how long you have been a believer; what matters is how thirsty and open you are. If we live in normal, trouble-free times, our thirst and openness may be minimal. During trouble, they can increase dramatically.

Patience and Perseverance

While we don't wish trouble on ourselves or our loved ones, **James 1:2** makes it clear that we should rejoice when we fall into diverse trials. But have you ever met anyone who did that in times of trouble? The injunction to praise God, despite our circumstances, is called the 'trying of our faith.' How much faith do you have? The truth is that you won't know until it is put to the test. How much do you know about history? You won't know until you take the final exam. Who are your real friends as opposed to the fair-weather version? You won't know until you're in trouble.

Affliction and trouble have an amazing ability to propel us into the presence of God, where mercy and grace await us (Hebrews 4:16).

Tested faith is strong faith. If it is wrongly directed, faith will fall flat on its face. When it's rightly directed to God and His Word, it will pass every test and win every prize. Just as weights build up muscle, so testing builds up faith.

The result of tested faith is patience. While it may not be the first thing on your wish list, the prudent person will embrace faith-induced patience. Why? It bestows staying power and perseverance, causes a greater maturity, and implies completion. As says **James 1:4** says: *"[L]et patience have her perfect work, that ye may be perfect and entire, wanting nothing."*

Increased Empathy

Experiencing challenges or pain and suffering also enables us to relate to, and empathise with, others who are suffering in a similar way. God can sometimes use our own experiences with poor health, unemployment, financial struggle, loss, or grief to provide practical support to others and

Eleven: God's Presence, Answered Prayer, and Enlargement

to minister to their needs in a deeply personal and more compassionate way.

Practical Steps to Manage our Troubles

Although suffering can draw us into a closer relationship with God, it can still take time to arrive at a place of understanding and acceptance in our life. Sometimes, it can be almost impossible to see any benefits when we are in the midst of difficult and painful situations, especially when they are not our fault. For example, how would we react to the premature loss of a beloved child or spouse? And how would a young mother, battling potentially terminal cancer, continue to stay strong in her faith when her heart yearns to be able to parent her small children and see them grow up? How do we remain thankful when we see one of our children struggling with serious mental health issues that are robbing them of their joy? In such cases, it is understandable that our natural urge is to cry out to the Lord to remove the cause of our suffering immediately because we are broken-hearted, or we see a loved one in pain.

In addition, there may be cases where we have contributed to the situation which is causing us pain. Yet it may be hard to acknowledge our role in this.

So what should we do? And how should we respond in a practical way to difficult circumstances? Here are some recommendations:

- Commit your trial and yourself to God and trust that He will effect the right outcome (Psalm 37:5);

- Remind yourself that you worship a most faithful God, who loves you unconditionally and is always true to His word. Revisit the promises of Psalm 91 and the gift of salvation. This will enable you to come boldly

God's Secret Place

unto God's throne of grace and seek His mercy and His grace in your time of need (Hebrews 4:16);

- Pray without ceasing (1 Thessalonians 5:17) and ask others to pray for you, too (1 Timothy 2:1). If you are uncertain about how to pray, there are many examples of prayers in Scripture including the Lord's prayer. But the Psalms also provide a wonderful source of inspiration on how to pray. Key elements are praise and thanksgiving as well as praying in accordance with God's will. We know that when we stand on the promises in God's Word, we pray in accordance with His will and we know, therefore, that our prayers will be heard (1 John 5:14-15). If you are unable to pray for yourself, ask others to stand in the gap on your behalf (Ezekiel 22:30);

- Fast if you wish to humble yourself before God and whole-heartedly seek His face because you need His help (2 Chronicles 7:14);

- Give God the honour and glory that are His due (Psalm 115:1; Matthew 5:16). Practise joyous, copious, and regular praise and worship, the language of faith. This cannot be emphasised enough (Psalm 150:6; 2 Chronicles 20:22). If this seems impossible at the time, try to read aloud Psalms of praise and see how the Holy Spirit will change your heart and bring peace where it might otherwise seem impossible;

- Search for, meditate upon, and speak out loud scriptures that remind you of God's nature and character and His extraordinary promises. Keep them in the midst of your heart. For God promises that His Word brings life to those who receive it and health to all their flesh (Proverbs 4:20-22). Doing this will also build your faith because we know that faith comes from hearing and hearing comes from the Word of God (Romans 10:17);

- Don't be afraid to tell God how you are feeling. If you're not sure how to do this, look to the psalms again for guidance. If you are struggling

Eleven: God's Presence, Answered Prayer, and Enlargement

to comprehend what is happening in your life, ask God to help you understand His ways (Psalm 25:4; 1 Corinthians 1:25); and ask Him to give you wisdom and understanding (Proverbs 4:7). God promises to give this to you generously without finding fault (1 James 5);

- If you think that there may be an issue in your life that might be impeding your ability to walk closely with God, such as anger, offence or unforgiveness, repent of that sin, ask God to give you insight, and try to learn the lessons that He might be showing you (1 John 1:8-10);

- Don't hesitate to seek spiritual support; but also try to stand on your own feet by doing what you can to draw closer to God (Galatians 6:2; Romans 15:1-2);

- Look for the grace mileposts along the way; they may first crop up at the beginning of the trial (Isaiah 30:21) and throughout; thank God when you see such mileposts (1 Thessalonians 5:18);

- Get the facts and know where you stand (John 8:31-32);

- Trust and keep trusting, no matter what (Proverbs 3:5-6; Psalm 37:3).

If you endeavour to love God, despite your circumstances, and practise obedience to His Word, God promises that He will never leave you nor forsake you. You will find a supernatural ability to persevere. And you will grow stronger in your faith and be capable of far more than you might ever have imagined.

Trouble's Greatest Benefit: Enlargement

It may not always seem like a consolation when we are in the midst of a crisis, but troubles also lead to enlargement. For believers, enlargement means growth, opportunity, and promotion. The Psalmist David acknowledged this when he cried out from the depths of his soul:

God's Secret Place

Hear me when I call, O God of my righteousness: thou hast enlarged me when I was in distress; have mercy upon me, and hear my prayer. (Psalm 4:1)

Few joys in life are greater than the feeling of a job well done. Whether it is faithful training that leads to winning the race, final exams which enable us to graduate, or completing an important project that benefits many, such achievements leave their mark. Those who have put in the work graduate to the next level.

Yet the pathway to promotion is never trouble-free. You can expect to encounter challenges along the way. Remember that these things are the pre-requisite to trouble's greatest benefit: enlargement.

Experiencing challenges or pain and suffering also enables us to relate to, and empathise with, others who are suffering in a similar way.

Enlargement is a worthy goal. Yet for enlargement even to be on the schedule, we have to be courageous, even adventurous, and willing. Willing to do what? Willing to step out of our comfort zone, away from what is familiar, comfortable, and safe, and begin to journey to a place we have never been before. If we want to fulfil the call of God in our lives, then there is no other way.

Are you satisfied with where you are at in life, or do you know in your heart of hearts that there is more? Is your present employment for life, or do you know that God has something else or something better? Are you growing spiritually where you're at, or is change looming ahead? Is the place where you live your home for life, or do you know a better place is waiting? Yesterday's circumstances, however positive, may not suffice for the future. There is so much more. We need to be enlarged.

Eleven: God's Presence, Answered Prayer, and Enlargement

Stepping out in God can bring temporal discomfort, but you will be rewarded with enlargement. Unwillingness to change or move on, when it is God's will for you to do so, will result in frustration and stagnation.

Biblical Examples of Enlargement

Abraham stepped out of his comfort zone when he left the cosmopolitan metropolis of Ur and headed to the backwaters of Canaan (Genesis 12:4).

Isaac stepped out of his comfort zone by remaining in Canaan when he wanted to go to Egypt (Genesis 26:2-6).

Jacob stepped out of his comfort zone when God commanded him to go to Egypt, but he dearly wanted to stay in Canaan (Genesis 46:1-7). The Bible provides many other examples, including the Galilean apostles of Jesus who loved to fish but instead went to the ends of the earth with the gospel. They became 'fishers of men.'

As David pronounced in **Psalm 4:1** above, God enlarged him, but not when things were going well, or when he behaved himself. Before David could be enlarged, he first had to experience distress. He became bigger and stronger as a result. So can we.

David's life is a catalogue of distresses, including but not limited to:

- Journeying in the wilderness with lions, bears, scorpions, and poisonous snakes while tending sheep (1 Samuel 17:34-37);

- Facing Goliath of Gath single-handedly (1 Samuel 17: 41-41);

- Fleeing for a protracted period from the face of Saul (1 Samuel 19-24; 26:1-25);

God's Secret Place

- Successful battles with Syrian, Moabites, Ammonites, Philistines, Amalek, and Zobah (2 Samuel 8:11-12); '

- Committing adultery with Bathsheba, the wife of another, and being rebuked by the prophet Nathan (2 Samuel 11-12);

- Facing serious family troubles and rebellion from his son Absalom (2 Samuel 15-18) as well as from Sheba the son of Bichri (2 Samuel 20);

- Enduring a deadly plague that was of his own making (2 Samuel 24:15-17).

Remarkably, David survived all these things and became enlarged. He could proclaim in **Psalm 18:19** that *"[God] brought me forth also into a large place; he delivered me, because he delighted in me."* After David was miraculously delivered from all his enemies, especially Saul, he jubilantly sang to the LORD that God had enlarged his steps under him so that his feet did not slip (2 Samuel 22:37). The mantle of enlargement was passed on from David to his son and successor, Solomon (1 Kings 4:29-34).

Similarly, Jabez prayed an immortal prayer that became the subject of a best-selling book by Dr. Bruce Wilkinson entitled *The Prayer of Jabez*. The heartfelt plea of Jabez is recorded in **1 Chronicles 4:10**:

> *Oh that thou wouldest bless me indeed, and enlarge my coast, and that thine hand might be with me, and that thou wouldest keep me from evil, that it may not grieve me! And God granted him that which he requested.*

Jabez wanted to be truly blessed by God. He was bold enough not to wait for enlargement; he prayed for it. This man of God would settle for nothing less than the hand of the Lord to be with him and keep him from evil. Without such oversight, evil might have beset Jabez and brought great grief to him, his loved ones, and even his nation.

Eleven: God's Presence, Answered Prayer, and Enlargement

Enlargement and God's Will

When you walk with God and yet sin, God will discipline you like a loving father (Proverbs 3:11-12). No discipline is pleasant, but it is far better than reaping the whirlwind of judgment. Even righteous people can experience distress that precedes enlargement, despite the fact that they have done nothing wrong. Imagine how much worse it is when a person has sinned. It is for these reasons that Jabez prayed the simple and powerful prayer above, which included a request that he be kept from evil. Apparently, God liked it for He granted Jabez the very thing he asked for.

Enlargement is not just a good idea; it is a divine command. After we read about our redemption through the suffering servant of **Isaiah 53** (Jesus the Messiah), we are commanded in the next chapter to sing and cry aloud (Isaiah 54:1) as a sign of giving birth. Then comes the command: enlarge the place of your tent and stretch the curtains of your habitation (54:2). You can feel the growing pains coming: enlarge, stretch, spare not, lengthen and strengthen - all these appear in one verse. It won't always be pleasant, but you will grow into a new dimension. As **Isaiah 54:3** promises, you will *"break forth"* on the right and left hand, and your descendants will inherit the nations and inhabit the desolate cities. This is enlargement, and all that you have to do is to pay a small price of distress to get there. Like the pains of a woman in labour, the process is not a pleasant one; but once it is over, you focus on the blessing, not the pain.

Honour from God (v. 15)

Psalm 91 promises answered prayer, divine presence in trouble, divine deliverance from trouble, and finally, in verse 15, honour from God Himself.

God's Secret Place

This world offers many prestigious honours, including Olympic gold medals, Academy Award Oscars, Nobel Peace Prizes, and a place on the Honours List. All these have merit but none can hold a candle to the greatest honour of all: that which comes from God. The Bible offers some superlative honours to those who believe. We learn that we are:

- Kings and priests to God (Revelation 1:6);

- Chosen from the foundation of the world (Ephesians 1:4);

- Ambassadors for Christ (2 Corinthians 5:20);

- A chosen generation, a royal priesthood, a holy nation, a special (peculiar) people (1 Peter 2:9);

- Saints of God (Ephesians 1:1; 2:19);

- Heirs of God, joint-heirs with Christ (Romans 8:17); and

- Blessed with all spiritual blessings in heavenly places (Ephesians 1:3).

When we have faced great loss, hardship, or even injustice at the hand of another, divine deliverance and honour are the greatest vindications of all for what we have endured. That is why we are urged not to avenge ourselves when we have been wronged. God can better handle weighty matters of this kind than we can, and He can do so without betraying His righteousness and justice.

Stepping out in God can bring temporal discomfort, but you will be rewarded with enlargement.

Leave the matter to God, and walk in the grace, power, and spirit of meekness. Remember that the most powerful men in the Bible - Moses and Jesus - were also the meekest. There is a lesson in this. Meekness

Eleven: God's Presence, Answered Prayer, and Enlargement

causes us - and our rights, vindications, methods, and motives - to decrease. But with Christ in us, the hope of glory increases. When we are meek, God will empower us, and we will walk in greater authority and anointing. God imposes His order on the world's disorder through us.

Enlargement is not just a good idea; it is a divine command.

Jesus, at His passion, was a textbook case of meekness. He did not resist arrest; did not respond to the lies spoken about Him; did not protest His innocence nor seek vindication; and he did not flinch when struck on the face nor lose control when condemned. But He held tight during the unspeakably painful ordeal of execution. Far from destroying Him and His infant movement, the Messiah's submission catapulted both Him and His church to prominence. Even by secular standards, Jesus Christ is the most influential person who ever lived. Yes, the meek shall inherit the earth (Psalm 37:11; Matthew 5:5).

Obedience and Service

Ultimately, honour from God belongs to those who obey and serve Him. Consider this Biblical hero. When he was perhaps no more than twenty years old, with the weight of the nation resting on his young shoulders, he watched as his father, an experienced soldier, king, and servant of God, struggled in the latter part of his reign with family and domestic rebellions. His older brother tried to usurp his power and take his throne and life from him. How could he, young and inexperienced as he was, hope to survive and thrive?

After coming to Gibeon, worshipping his father's God, and offering a thousand burnt offerings, this young man went to bed. That evening, God graciously visited him in a dream and told him that he could ask God for anything that he wanted (1 Kings 3:5).

God's Secret Place

Think about it. If you could ask God for something, anything, with full assurance that it would be granted on the spot, what would it be - riches, fame, acclaim, vindication, or health and longevity? But what did our hero ask for? Nothing like this. Instead, he sought the very thing that would help him to serve God better. He asked for *"an understanding heart to judge [God's] people"* so that he might *"discern between good and bad"* and lead the great nation of Israel (1 Kings 3:9,12).

Remember that the most powerful men in the Bible - Moses and Jesus - were also the meekest.

The king in question was Solomon. God was very pleased with his request and granted it immediately. He gave him *"a wise and an understanding heart"* and promised that there would never be anyone like him, either before or after him (v.12). The young king became 'the wisest man who ever lived,' humanly speaking. Yet as we learn in the **Book of Proverbs**, authored by Solomon, wisdom comes into our lives bearing gifts. God gave Solomon the great things that he had not asked for: riches and honour (1 Kings 3:13). His renown was so great that it attracted the visit of an admiring, Oriental queen from the faraway land of Sheba (1 Kings 10).

Psalm 91 promises immeasurable benefits to those who love and obey God. That is what we are called to do. In **Matthew 7:21-23**, the Lord Jesus Christ warns that only those who do the will of the heavenly Father shall enter into the kingdom of heaven. Obedience is the key. Merely giving lip service to His Lordship is not enough. But if we do obey, the rewards are great.

Jesus reiterates this message in **John 12:26** when he says:

> *If any man serve me, let him follow me; and where I am, there shall also my servant be: if any man serve me, him will my Father honour.*

Eleven: God's Presence, Answered Prayer, and Enlargement

His message is simple: obey God, serve God, and, by so doing, honour God. And those who honour God, God will honour in return. Honour from people lasts for a time; honour from God lasts for eternity.

Now, more than ever, it is time to trust God with all of your heart, all of the time, especially during testing. He will make a way for you, even when there seems to be no way.

So let us turn now to the closing verses of Psalm 91; and let us look more closely at the new, improved life which God promises those who place their trust in Him.

---

[i] *Footprints in the Sand* by Mary Stevenson. http://www.footprints-inthe-sand.com/index.php?page=Poem/Poem.php. Accessed 6 August 2022.

CHAPTER TWELVE

The Power of an Endless Life

Who is made, not after the law of a carnal commandment, but after the power of an endless life - **Hebrews 7:16**.

With long life will I satisfy him, and shew him my salvation -**Psalm 91:16**.

As we get to verse 16 - the final verse of this majestic psalm - we see that it promises longevity and salvation. These promises are inseparable. We can only have longevity with God and His saints forever through salvation in Christ. Salvation connects us perpetually with God, the source of all life. At the same time, salvation saves us from divine wrath, which entails punishment and permanent separation from God. As **Romans 5:9** says: *"Much more then, being now justified by his blood, we shall be saved from wrath through him."*

So longevity and salvation are what this chapter is about.

Long Life

Psalm 91 promises the gift of long life. But let's put this promise in context. In much of the Old Testament, there was very little understanding of life after death. For many, the final destination of the dead was *Sheol* (Hebrew) or *hades* (Greek), a most unhappy place in the underworld realm.[i]

In the story of the rich man and Lazarus in **Luke 16**, both men were in *Sheol/hades* but found it was compartmentalised. Lazarus the beggar was in bliss in the presence of father Abraham, the man of faith and friend of

God. The ungodly rich man was in torment. They could see each other, but the chasm between them was too big to cross.

Fortunately for the redeemed, the situation with Sheol/hades changed radically for the better after the resurrection and ascension of Christ. Believers no longer go to the underworld; they go immediately to be with God in heaven (see Luke 20:37; 23:43; John 14:2; 2 Corinthians 5:1, 5, 6, 8; Philippians 1:23; 1 Peter 1:3-5; 5:10-11). These verses speak about existence for believers after our natural life ends, including eternal life, great joy, preparation of a place for us, and deliverance from suffering and evil.

Old Testament Mindset

But let us return to the Old Testament mindset. Given that there was a very limited understanding of the afterlife, the best one could hope for was a long, healthy, happy life in this world. Longevity was more desirable than a vague existence in the underworld after death.

The earlier characters in Genesis had enormously long lives; the lives of the three patriarchs Abraham, Isaac, and Jacob were still lengthy but less so. As the Old Testament continued, lifespans decreased notably. Longevity was viewed as a gift or blessing from God. By contrast, a life cut short, particularly in a violent and/or untimely manner, was considered a curse from God.

Meditating on the Word

Psalm 91 promises longevity, but how do you get it? If you review ten famous verses on the subject, you may be surprised to learn that the normal methods of life enhancement and extension are not there. There is no mention of diet, exercise, weight training, organic food, vitamin supplements, or yoga. Remember that since long life is a gift from God, it

Twelve: The Power of an Endless Life

behoves us to listen to what He - who has no beginning or end and is called the Ancient of Days - has to say on the matter (Daniel 7:9-14). He has the power of an endless life.

When you learn and meditate upon the Word of God and nurture it in your heart, God promises to multiply your days and the days of your children. In addition, both you and your children will dwell in the land promised to Abraham, Isaac, and Jacob (Deuteronomy 11:21). Elsewhere in Deuteronomy, the willingness to walk in God's ways also attracts the promise of long life in the land of promise (5:33).[ii]

Half the references to longevity are found in the **Book of Proverbs**. Can you guess what the key ingredient is? Not surprisingly, it is wisdom. Learning and keeping God's commandments 'in the heart' delivers and multiplies long life and peace (Proverbs 3:2). But what does the world seek after? The usual wish list includes riches, fame, acclaim, and a long, healthy life.

Amazingly, taking hold of divine wisdom delivers the same outcomes but without the bitter aftertaste. **Proverbs 3:16** tells us, *"Length of days is in her right hand; and in her left hand riches and honour."* The 'her' in this verse is 'wisdom' personified. Think about it: the riches, longevity, and honour obtained by the ungodly and foolish are a poor substitute for wisdom's version of these coveted things.

Listening to, comprehending, and obeying God's Word and making the pursuit of wisdom and understanding your highest priority mean that the years of your life will be many (Proverbs 4:10). Similarly, in **Proverbs 9:11**, we see that wisdom's promise of long life is granted to those who cooperate with her.

God's Secret Place

Fear of the Lord

All the Biblical ingredients for longevity are interwoven one with another. Another feature, related to the earlier ones, is the *"fear of the Lord"* (Proverbs 9:10). We never tire of invoking this time-honoured exhortation. But once we embrace it, we are connected with God, dwell in His shadow, hear His voice, feed at His table, enjoy His presence and protection, and are delivered from all other fears. Masterfully, 'fear of the Lord' is called *"the beginning of wisdom"* (9:10). Godly fear should be pre-eminent in our lives because it leads to unequalled benefits. It is also the great watershed between life and eternity. Those who reject it run the risk that their lives will be cut short, both from a natural/physical and a spiritual perspective. Those who wisely embrace it are promised that their days *"shall be multiplied'* and *"the years of [their] life increased"* (9:11). There is no in-between, middle ground. It is either the fear of the Lord or carnal folly.

In Solomon's case, God promised him long life, but this blessing came with a condition: he would have to walk in God's ways and keep his statutes and commandments, as his father David did (1 Kings 3:14). Unfortunately, Solomon fell short and did not attain even the years of his father. He missed out on longevity because he did not follow God with all of his heart, all of the time.

Speaking No Evil

One of the best, life-extending pieces of advice we can find comes from **1 Peter 3:10**, which quotes from **Psalm 34:12-16**. In these parallel passages, longevity is connected to what comes out of our mouth, not by what goes into it. If you love to live and want to see many good days, then watch what you say. Stop speaking evil and keep your lips from guile.

Guile can be defined as cunning, clever, devious, and often dishonest words or behaviour.[iii] It is rife today in our increasingly deceptive world.

Twelve: The Power of an Endless Life

That's why being a person without guile is exceptional. It was this very trait that attracted Nathanael to Jesus and vice versa. In **John 1:47**, the Lord identified him as an *"Israelite indeed in whom [there] is no guile."*

In other places, Jesus also highlighted the principle that what goes into the mouth does not defile a person, but that which comes out of the mouth does because it *"come[s] forth from the heart"* (Matthew 15:10-20; Mark 7:18-23).

To sum up, we learn that longevity comes from fear of the Lord, and wisdom is derived from that fear (Proverbs 9:10); it also comes from obedience to the Word and keeping your mouth clean and sweet.

The Coming of Jesus and the Promise of Life-Everlasting

But since the death and resurrection of Jesus, we no longer have to fear death. As the Messiah of the world, Jesus died a slow yet violent death on a cursed cross to redeem us from our sins. We see this confirmed in **Galatians 3:13** where Paul writes: *"Christ hath redeemed us from the curse of the law, being made a curse for us: for it is written, Cursed is every one that hangeth on a tree."*[iv]

Now that Christ's mission of redeeming humanity has been accomplished, the notion of longevity takes on a new perspective. New Testament believers may or may not live a long, natural life; but all are promised *"the power of an endless life"* (Hebrews 7:16). Logically, life forever is far more important than earthly longevity. After all, what's the benefit of a long life here on earth if an individual then faces an eternity without God?

Life does not cease when the heart stops beating and we no longer breathe. It continues in the presence of God (2 Corinthians 5:1, 2, 8). God is the God of the living for those who believe in Him (Luke 20:38). Faith

God's Secret Place

in the gospel causes believers to live before God today, tomorrow, and forever.

When A Believer's Life is Cut Short

But what about those who come to Christ and walk in obedience and wisdom, yet do not live long lives? It does happen. There is a moving story of a sixteen-year-old Christian girl who attended a large church. This teenager was the only Christian in her family. She had a great testimony and found favour with all people. To a confidant, she shared that the salvation of her family was so important to her that she was willing to give her life in order to see them receive the gospel.

There is no in-between, middle ground, or no-man's land. It is either the fear of the Lord or carnal folly.

Her wish was granted. At a youth outing at the beach, she was wading in the waves with another young person. A rogue wave came and took her, and her alone, out to sea. Shortly afterwards, her lifeless body was washed back onto the shore. Understandably, her unchurched family were beside themselves with grief and were tempted to blame the church for her death. But not long after, they came to faith in Christ.

What can we make of this? As always, we need to try to see things from a divine, long-term, Biblical perspective. Earthly longevity, in good health and peace, is a great gift, but a far more important blessing is eternal life. When we comprehend the nature of the afterlife and eternity, we will better understand what Paul meant when he wrote: *"We are ... willing rather to be absent from the body, and to be present with the Lord"* (2 Corinthians 5:8). He could say this because he considered that *"to live is Christ, and to die is gain"* (Philippians 1:21); and for that reason, he had *{a} desire to depart, and be with Christ; which is far better'* (Philippians 1:23).

Twelve: The Power of an Endless Life

The promise of eternal life can offer consolation and hope to those who are grieving. If you are recovering from bereavement, it may help comfort you if you can take to heart what we know lies ahead for us as believers. In **2 Corinthians 4:17-18**, Paul writes that if you could only see into the invisible but eternal realm, you would know that God is working for you a *"far more exceeding and eternal weight of glory"* (v. 17). So if you can, try not to place your trust in the visible, temporal realm; make your focus on God the Eternal One. He invites you to cast all your cares and grief onto Him for He cares for you (1 Peter 5:7).

The Power of an Endless Life

The promise of eternal life is grand but, at times, difficult to comprehend because we live in a world order that is full of sin and death. Yet thanks to the Holy Spirit and the Word of God, we can comprehend the *'power of an endless life'* in a way that the world cannot. Think of eternity as a grand family reunion.

We see a glimpse of this in **Hebrews 12:22-24**. There we learn that we will encounter God; the Lord Jesus Christ, the mediator of the new covenant; innumerable angels in festal gathering; the assembly of the firstborn enrolled in heaven; and the spirits of the righteous people made perfect. This may be the same thing as the *"cloud of witnesses"* mentioned in **Hebrews 12:1**.

When you eventually encounter wonderful people, including your redeemed loved ones and the heavenly hosts, any pain and heaviness that you may be experiencing now will be forgotten. The glorious promises in **Revelation 21:4** will come to pass:

> *God shall wipe away all tears from [our] eyes; and there shall be no more death, neither sorrow, nor crying, neither shall there be any more pain: for the former things are passed away.*

We will enjoy a sense of collective amnesia in respect of former painful, temporal things when encountering the power of an endless life and the glory of eternity.

However, we need to understand the afterlife better. In **John 11:25-26**, Jesus makes a bold claim when He says:

> *I am the resurrection, and the life: he that believeth in me, though he were dead, yet shall he live: And whosoever liveth and believeth in me shall never die.*

Here Jesus is saying that the dead shall live again, and the believer shall never die. If this weren't true, it would be absurdly audacious.

But what does Christ mean by these words? What does He mean by saying that believers shall pass from death to life and never die? To answer this question, we need to understand the nature of death. For the average person, death means the cessation of breathing and vital organ function. The body lies still and becomes stone cold. The person is pronounced 'dead.' Jesus has something else in mind, and it is worth comprehending.

The Meaning of Death

Death, in its simplest sense, means 'separation.' The personal human spirit separates from the physical body, and this brings death (**James 2:26**). The deceased is 'separated' from loved ones in the land of the living. Fundamentally, death means *'separation from the source of life.'* What or who is the source of life? It is Almighty God and Jesus Christ, *"the Prince of life"* (Acts 3:15).

God told Adam and Eve that on the day that they ate the fruit from *"the tree of the knowledge of good and evil,"* they would *"surely die"* (Genesis 2:17). Contrary to the divine command, the first couple did eat of the

Twelve: The Power of an Endless Life

fruit. But what happened on that day? Did they eat the fruit and then promptly drop dead? No, they did not.

Adam and Eve lived and breathed for many years to come. So what happened on the dreadful day of The Fall when their idyllic world - and ours - went rogue? Their sin separated them from God and His presence. They no longer had close communion with the Almighty; they no longer lived in the garden that He had made for them; and they no longer had His favour on their lives. We learn that long, hard labour by day and travail pains in childbirth were both parts of the curse that resulted from their disobedience (Genesis 3:16-20). Death was also a central part of that curse.

Earthly longevity, in good health and peace, is a great gift, but a far more important blessing is eternal life.

Although Adam and Eve's connection with God was not completely severed because their sons Cain and Abel offered sacrifices to God, the fact is that they were spiritually dead; they were separated from God's presence, plan, and kingdom. Unless that state of spiritual death is remedied *in this life*, the danger is that one will enter into eternal death from which there is no escape.

That's where Christ and the gospel come in. By faith, we receive Christ's atoning work on the cross and the power of His glorious resurrection. Then the new birth cancels out the condition of spiritual death in this world and delivers us from eternal death in the world to come. The *"law of the Spirit of life in Christ Jesus"* makes us *"free from the law of sin and death"* (Romans 8:2).

But let's go back to Jesus's words in **John 8:51** that the man who keeps His sayings *"shall never see death."* For 2,000 years, faithful and true Christians have lived and died. Is there a contradiction? No, there is not. There is a wonderful explanation.

In **Revelation 6:7-8**, we have a brief description of the fourth horseman of the apocalypse.[v] He rides on a pale horse; the rider is called *"Death"* and *"Hell"* follows with him. In other words, death is described as a person.

The Intermediate State

The state of a believer in between their physical death and physical resurrection is called the 'intermediate state.' At the very end, we will enter the 'eternal state' where the New Jerusalem becomes our permanent home (Revelation 21:1-22:5).[vi] But when a believer's natural life comes to an end and they shut their eyes for the last time, what happens when they open them for the first time on the other side? Whom does he or she see in the intermediate state? We learn that when believers are absent from the body, they are present with the Lord (2 Corinthians 5:8).

So it is safe to say that when believers' eyes open on the other side in eternity, they will be looking at the face of Jesus. They cannot and will not see death, the fourth horseman of the apocalypse (Revelation 6:8). For unbelievers, it is a different story. While we do not know exactly what happens in detail, it seems probable that somehow, someway, they will encounter the rider of the pale horse.

Our Future Resurrection

A powerful principle about being alive to God in the intermediate state comes from the story of the Sadducees who asked Jesus an insincere and hypocritical question in **Matthew 22:23-33**. The Sadducees were Jewish aristocrats, who did not believe in the resurrection of the dead themselves but knew that Jesus did. Despite this, they queried, hypothetically, what would be the position of a childless woman, married consecutively to seven brothers. Whose wife would she be in the resurrection?

Twelve: The Power of an Endless Life

Jesus rightly rebuked the Sadducees for being in error because they did not know the Scriptures or the power of God (Matthew 22:29). He went on to say that in the resurrection, people will not marry nor will they be given in marriage; rather, they will be like the angels in heaven (v. 30). After all, there will be no need for procreation within marriage since people will be living eternally.

To further prove to these sceptical Sadducees that there would be a future resurrection of the dead, Jesus then drew on the celebrated Old Testament story where God first appeared to Moses and spoke to him from the burning bush. It was on this occasion that God declared Himself to be the God of his ancestors, the patriarchs (Exodus 3:6). It is worth setting out all that Jesus said in **Matthew 22:31-32**:

> *But as touching the resurrection of the dead, have ye not read that which was spoken unto you by God, saying, I am the God of Abraham, and the God of Isaac, and the God of Jacob? God is not the God of the dead, but of the living.*

Why did Jesus choose to highlight the conversation God had with Moses and why is it so significant? When God said that He is "the God of Abraham," He did not say, 'I **was** the God of Abraham, but he is dead now so I am not his God anymore.' Instead, God spoke in the present tense, declaring Himself to be the God of the patriarchs, who were still alive in His presence, though they had been physically deceased for centuries. Jesus, therefore, was able to conclude that *"God is not the God of the dead, but of the living"* (Matthew 22:32). As far as God is concerned, this means that even if people are physically dead, they are still alive in Him.

Unlike the Sadducees, Jesus understood that this was all due to God's eternality: that is, His pre-existence in the past, His power in the present, and His total claim to possess and rule the future. This is reflected in the name God gave Himself when Moses asked God how he should describe

Him to the children of Israel. *"Thus shalt thou say unto [them], I AM hath sent me unto you"* (Exodus 3:14).

As we have already seen, I AM is the divine name. It signifies that God was, God is, and God will always be, the Almighty (Revelation 1:8).

Every claim that Jesus ever made is based on this extraordinary fact. Because of God's eternality, Jesus can be called the *"prince of life"* (Acts 3:15), and He has been able to abolish death (2 Timothy 1:10).

So when Jesus says you are alive and will never die, remember that this means that your new birth has connected you to the source of life. You are no longer spiritually dead but spiritually alive. No longer do you face the prospect of eternal death. You are alive to God. Nothing, but nothing, can separate you from God and life, not even death itself. This is what gave the apostle Paul the confidence to declare in **Romans 8:38-39**:

> *I am persuaded, that neither **death, nor life**, neither angels nor principalities, nor powers, nor thing present, nor things to come, no height, nor depth, nor any other creature shall be able to separate us from the love of God, which is in Christ Jesus our Lord.* (emphasis mine)

For this, we can truly say, Hallelujah!

The Salvation of God

We are now in the last part of the final verse of **Psalm 91**. God has already promised long life, and now we go to the 'big ticket' item: an unambiguous and comprehensive presentation of the salvation of the Lord. Indeed, 'longevity' and 'salvation' are a major part of God's plan for you; without them, there is no eternity with the Almighty.

Twelve: The Power of an Endless Life

As we have learned, long life is not just limited to the natural life; it is an allusion to the gift of eternal life. What life is longer than the life that never ends? What power is greater than the power of an endless life?

The Meaning of Salvation

What does the word 'salvation' really mean? Salvation, in its simplest sense, means to be delivered from great danger. **Psalm 107** speaks of salvation from a great storm and guidance to our desired haven (v. 30). Angelic deliverance also brought salvation from prison for Peter (Acts 5:18-20; 12:7-10) as well as Paul and Silas (Acts 16:25-32).

Salvation was always God's will for Israel and the nations. **Isaiah 45:17** tells us this:

> *Israel shall be saved in the LORD with an everlasting salvation: ye shall not be ashamed nor confounded world without end.*[vii]

The Book of Isaiah is especially focused on the theme of salvation. Isaiah's Hebrew name is *Yesha-Yahu* - the Lord is my salvation. *Yesha* is another form of the name *'Yeshua.'* We know that when it comes to Jesus Christ (Hebrews 2:3), He offers a great salvation, indeed, the greatest possible.

Nothing, but nothing, can separate you from God and life, not even death itself.

Our great Saviour offers a salvation that delivers us from every conceivable foe. There are at least seven adversaries from which He saves us. These include:

- **Sin**: As we learned, Jesus' proper name in Hebrew is 'Yeshua,' which means 'saviour' because He saves His people from their sins (Matthew 1:21).

- **Sickness**: Jesus had a perfect, sinless body, but He was wounded, bruised, crucified, and died so that by His stripes we might be healed (Isaiah 53:5). That's why, in His name and by faith in His name, we are made whole in every respect (Acts 3:16).

- **Danger**: Isn't that what **Psalm 91** is about?

- **The world and worldliness**: Clinging to the things of the world is like clinging to the deck chairs of the ocean liner Titanic after it hit the iceberg. Worldliness does not enhance life but ruins everything it touches. Jesus tells us to be of good cheer because he has overcome the world (John 16:33; Romans 8:6, 8, 11-13).

- **The devil** (1 John 3:8): The devil is powerful and pervasive, but he is no match for Jesus. Having destroyed his works, Jesus passed on His authority to us. That's why **James 4:7** tells us to resist the devil and he will flee from us. This would not have been possible unless Jesus had done His great saving work first. Since He overcame the devil, so can we.

- **Death**: We have already covered this point, but death does not destroy us nor separate us from God. We have eternal life now and, in the intermediate state, we have it even more. After the resurrection, we can never die again physically or spiritually. Death is still an enemy but a defeated one (1 Corinthians 15:25-26, 54-57).

- **Hell** (Revelation 20:14): Hell is real but heaven can be yours. Christ loved you enough to offer you a way out from hell. Though there can be debate about the full meaning of 'hell,' what is not debatable is that those who accept the free gift of the gospel will not experience it.

All seven of the enemies listed above are formidable. We could never defeat them on our own. The majesty and glory of Jesus Christ, Son of

Twelve: The Power of an Endless Life

David and Son of God, is that He has defeated all seven foes. That's why He is a great saviour, and our salvation is great too.

In **Psalm 91**, you learn that you need to live a life of reverent submission and trust in God at all times. When you do so, you are assured of grace, peace, and protection in this world as well as the promise of the world to come. Now is the time, during relative peace and prosperity, to take the exhortations of Psalm 91 and put them into practice. Make God your refuge and fortress. Otherwise, you will find life in this present evil age to be overwhelming.

Salvation - What Does it Involve?

The salvation of God through the gospel of Christ is beyond price. You cannot earn it, purchase it, nor deserve it. The only thing you can do is to repent and receive it by faith. As the verses in **Ephesians 2: 8-9** so wonderfully summarise, we are saved by the grace of God via faith. It is God's grace that is the bedrock of salvation (Titus 2:11), and it is accessed by our faith. Think of saving grace as subterranean fresh water, and faith as the pipe and pump that accesses and brings it to the surface. There is plenty of grace to save everyone, but only those who exercise faith will obtain it. Paul and Silas confirmed this when they told the Philippian jailer in **Acts 16:31**: *"Believe on the Lord Jesus Christ, and thou shalt be saved, and thy house."* It is so simple that even a child can understand it and many do.

This salvation is not only for God's chosen people the Jews but also for all other non-Jewish people, namely, the Gentiles. Paul - the 'Hebrew of Hebrews' yet apostle to the Gentiles - tells us that God's salvation is available to all nations through faith (Galatians 3:8-9). As we saw earlier, when people say 'Yes' to the gospel, they become 'children of Abraham' and heirs according to the promise (Galatians 3:29).

Gospel salvation is an urgent message: call on the name of the Lord and you shall be saved. But you cannot call on the Lord until you first believe in Him. You cannot believe in Him until you have heard the good news. And you cannot hear the good news unless someone tells you (Romans 10:14-17).

Cornelius, the Roman centurion from Caesarea, was an exceptional man. He was sincere, pious, and generous; yet despite his many good deeds, he still needed to be saved. That's why the angel directed Cornelius in **Acts 11:13-14** to send for Peter in Joppa so that he could hear how he and all his household could be saved.

The gospel of salvation is simple, straightforward, grace-filled, faith-accessed, and pressing. We need to share it whenever we can. Whatever our calling or spiritual gift, we can still heed the words of Paul to 'Pastor Timothy' in **2 Timothy 4:5** to *"do the work of an evangelist."*

Salvation in Action: A Case Study

Salvation is promised and that is a great gift. But what does salvation look like? How can we get the genuine version rather than a poor substitute? These vital questions deserve an answer, and it comes from the Bible of course.

In **Luke 19:1-10**, we find the amusing yet heart-warming story of a chief tax collector called Zacchaeus from Jericho. People in this profession were greatly despised by the general population; after all, who loves the tax man? In Jesus' day, the tax collector worked for the Romans and represented the hated occupiers of the land of Israel. A second strike against them was that they often abused their position by menacing the population and/or taking more than required while keeping the difference. It was a corrupt vocation, and Zacchaeus would have done well to lie low. Yet it was people like him (and other obvious sinners

Twelve: The Power of an Endless Life

such as drunkards and harlots) who were far more attracted to Christ than the religious elite. Zacchaeus was no exception.

However, there was a great stir in the community. Jesus of Nazareth was coming through town. The tax collector did not want to miss out, but he had a problem. He was short of stature and couldn't see Jesus because of the great crowd. Not to be left behind, Zacchaeus climbed up a sycamore tree to see the Lord pass by. It was like a balcony view.

The gospel of salvation is simple, straightforward, grace-filled, faith-accessed, and pressing.

Then something remarkable happened. As Jesus walked by, He looked up at the tree, saw Zacchaeus, called him by name, and told him to come down so He could stay at his home. From then on, Zacchaeus would conduct himself as one who had received the Lord's salvation.

First, he came down the tree quickly. People who are coming to God do not drag the chain; they respond promptly. Then it says that he received Jesus joyfully (Luke 19:6). It is a joy to come to Jesus, and it is a misery to reject him. Despised, dishonoured, outcast Zacchaeus had great joy that the religious elite knew nothing about. Third, Zacchaeus let Jesus into his home. That is always a wise thing to do, but it does not stop there. Jesus needs to be in your home, your head (mind), and your heart. Solid evidence exists that for Zacchaeus, Jesus was in all three places.

After the meal, Zacchaeus made a grand and public announcement. A very wealthy man, he promised to give half of his goods to the poor. In addition, he would give four times the amount to anyone who had been defrauded by him.

In response to these actions, Jesus made the wonderful, life-changing announcement to Zacchaeus: *"This day is salvation come to this house,*

God's Secret Place

forsomuch as he also is a son of Abraham. For the Son of man is come to seek and to save that which was lost" (Luke 19:9-10).

Signs of Repentance and Walking with God

Repentance toward God, faith in the gospel, and confessing Christ activates saving faith, and all this leads to salvation (Acts 20:21; Romans 10:9; Hebrews 6:1). So the chief tax collector of the Israelite city of Jericho now had salvation in Christ. In addition to accepting Christ's invitation promptly and joyfully, Zacchaeus demonstrated his repentance and faith. How? He showed what John the Baptist called *"fruits worthy of repentance"* (Luke 3:8). Talk is cheap and lip service vain; it is action that counts. Zacchaeus' willingness to offload part of his fortune tells us that he substituted heavenly pleasure for worldly treasure (Matthew 6:21; Luke 12:34). When people feel genuine sorrow for their sins and take action to make it right, this is the fruit that God looks for.

Zacchaeus's response can be contrasted with that of the rich young ruler. Both men were wealthy and loved by Jesus, and both were given a personalised invitation to follow Him. Part of the deal, in their cases, was to divest some or all of their fortune. Zacchaeus did so joyfully since there is great joy in obedience. The rich young ruler declined Jesus' offer to follow Him and walked away grieving because he did not wish to part with his riches (Matthew 19:16-22; Mark 10:17-22; Luke 18:18-23).

Jesus called Zacchaeus a 'son of Abraham.' He may already have been an ethnic son but now he would be one spiritually as well. Those who are 'sons of Abraham' do what Abraham would do (John 8:39-40). What did Abraham do that determined who his sons would be?

1. Abraham was a man of faith; he believed God, and it was credited to him as righteousness (Genesis 15:6);

Twelve: The Power of an Endless Life

2. Abraham walked with the Lord and was called the friend of God (2 Chronicles 20:7; James 2:23);

3. Like Zacchaeus, Abraham obeyed God promptly. For example, Abraham and his men were circumcised on the very day God gave the command (Genesis 17:23; 26). And he hastily packed his bags to take Isaac to the land of Moriah when God spoke to him (Genesis 22:2-3).

Could there be any greater accolade in life than to be called the faithful friend of God?

Zacchaeus' willingness to offload part of his fortune tells us that he substituted heavenly pleasure for worldly treasure (Matthew 6:21; Luke 12:34).

We have just experienced a great adventure in the timeless **Psalm 91**. To reach God's safe space, we have learned that it is not a matter of geography and transport but of faith and obedience. The promise of God's protective presence becomes very real. Yet ultimately, the best earthly refuge is, at best, a way station to God's ultimate 'secret place' – the heavenly city, the New Jerusalem (Revelation 21:1-22:5). It is the city *"with foundations whose builder and maker is God"* (Hebrews 11:10). Coming to Christ means coming, eventually, to His capital city, *"the heavenly Jerusalem"* (Hebrews 12:22). Paul calls this *"Jerusalem ... above"* the *"mother of us all"* (Galatians 4:26).

The New Jerusalem

There are 1,189 chapters in the Bible and only two of them are devoted to the eternal state and its holy city.[viii]

God's Secret Place

It is no coincidence that it is called the New Jerusalem. It is called 'New' because it replaces the existing Jerusalem – the finite, sin-stained, troubled city of stone that has been in great bondage to her children, even today. It is called 'Jerusalem' because Jesus is the son and heir of King David (Matthew 21:9; Revelation 5:5); He will sit on David's throne in the *"City of David"* (2 Samuel 5:7), known also as the *"city of the great King"* (Psalm 48:2; Matthew 5:35). Just as the old Jerusalem was David's City, so is the New Jerusalem the city of the son of David.[ix]

New Jerusalem is the centrepiece of the 'eternal state,' the final and endless era of our existence, the *"forever and ever, Amen"* (Revelation 7:12). The Apostle John describes it as *"coming down from heaven from God, prepared as a bride adorned for her husband"* (Revelation 21:2). The description of this metropolis, which will be made in heaven but deployed on earth (Revelation 21:1), is glorious. But what makes the New Jerusalem even more wonderful are 18 things that will not be in it.

In the Eternal State, there will be no more:

1. Death (Rev. 20:14; 21:4);
2. Hades (20:14);
3. Sea (21:1);
4. Sorrow (21:4);
5. Crying (21:4);
6. Pain (21:4);
7. Cowardice (21:8);
8. Unbelieving (21:8);
9. Abominable (21:8);
10. Murderers (21:8);
11. Sexually immoral (21:8);
12. Sorcerers (21:8);
13. Idolaters (21:8);
14. Liars (21:8);
15. Temple (21:22);

Twelve: The Power of an Endless Life

16. Night (21:25);
17. Curse (22:3);
18. Dogs (22:15).

Just the absence of these things alone will make the new city without a peer. The pain, torment, and fear of today will be forgotten; and death, sorrow, crying, and pain will pass away (Revelation 21:4). Jesus promises to *"make all things new"* (v. 5).

Most importantly, we learn that *"the tabernacle of God [will be] with men, and He will dwell with them, and they shall be His people"* (Revelation 21:3). This means that we will be living in God's presence, and God Himself will be with us and be our God (Revelation 21:3). When you think about it, this New Jerusalem is God's ultimate secret place and when it happens, the secret will be a secret no more.

For this reason, it is worth keeping our eyes on Christ and this extraordinary prize. God's best is worth the perseverance and the wait. We cannot imagine the grandeur and glory of eternity offered to us as sons and daughters of the living God. So let us join with the Holy Spirit and say, *"Come, Lord Jesus"* (Revelation 22:17, 20).

But until that day, we can still access God's protection, guidance, and peace on earth. God offers us the opportunity to be safely led by Christ, the good shepherd, to the secret place of **Psalm 91** where we can find rest, despite the most challenging of circumstances.

God's secret place is waiting for you.

God's Secret Place

[i] Numerous verses speak about hell (*sheol, hades*); here are the references: Deuteronomy 32:22; 2 Samuel 22:6; Job 11:8; 26:6; Psalm 9:17; 16:10; 18:5; 55:15; 86:13; 116:3; 139:8; Proverbs 5:5; 7:27; 9:18; 15:11; 15:24; 23:14; 27:20; Isaiah 5:14; 14:9, 15; 28:15, 18; 57:9; Ezekiel 31:16, 17; 32:21, 27; Amos 9:2; Jonah 2:2; Habakkuk 2:5; Matthew 5:22, 29, 30; 10:28; 11:23; 16:18; 18:9; 23:15; 23:33; Mark 9:43, 45, 47; Luke 10:15; 12:5; 16:23; Acts 2:27, 31; James 3:6; 2 Peter 2:4.

[ii] As an aside, you may wonder how the latter promise of dwelling in the land applies to Gentiles? This is a big topic, beyond the scope of this book, but remember this: our future eternal home - for redeemed Jews and redeemed Gentiles - is called the New Jerusalem (Revelation 21:1-22:5).

[iii] 'Guile,' *Compact Oxford English Dictionary of Current English - Third Edition*, Oxford University Press 2005, 448.

[iv] Deuteronomy 21:22-23 which says that God places a curse on those who are hanged on a tree.

[v] *Apocalypse* is the Greek name for the Book of Revelation. It means 'uncovering,' 'unveiling,' 'revealing.' "G602 - apokalypsis - Strong's Greek Lexicon (kjv)." Blue Letter Bible. Accessed 20 Aug, 2022. https://www.blueletterbible.org/lexicon/g602/kjv/tr/0-1/.

[vi] Again, the study of eschatology is large. Our physical resurrection happens when Christ comes for us (1 Thessalonians 4); He has a 1,000 year earthly reign called the Millennium (Revelation 20); followed by the eternal state (Revelation 21-22). For now, let's continue to focus on the intermediate state.

[vii] Other passages in Isaiah speak of God's reaching out to the Gentiles or saving the Gentiles. See Isaiah 11:10; 42:1,6; 49:6; 54:3; 60:3; 62:2.

[viii] Kameel Majdali, *White Horse Coming: Seven Keys to Understanding the Book of Revelation,* Melbourne: Teach All Nations, 2017, 163.

Without complicating matters further regarding eschatology, the Millennial reign of Christ, son of David, mentioned in Revelation 20, will be in the post-tribulation Old Jerusalem. After the one-thousand-year reign, the New Jerusalem will descend out of heaven (Revelation 21) and become our eternal home.

Appendix One

A Psalm 91 Prayer

As we come to the end of this book, the following is a prayer you can pray to begin your long-term sojourn in the best refuge imaginable, this side of heaven.

Heavenly Father,

I come to You in the mighty Name of Jesus; I praise and glorify your holy name. Thank you for the many benefits you bestow on me.

I acknowledge that I, my nation, and the world are in trouble. These are challenging days and many have no hope. Yet - praise God - you offer rock-solid eternal hope, through Jesus Christ my Lord.

As for me, Lord, I approach You in humility and faith: humility because I know that I am not capable of solving these problems on my own; and faith because I trust that You will come close to me as I come close to you;[i] and I know that you will answer my prayer.[ii]

I thank You for Psalm 91 and the secret place. I know that it is more real than anything this world can offer. As an act of my will, in faith, I declare that I have entered the "secret place of the most High." So, in that spirit of faith, I declare that You, O Lord, are my refuge, my fortress, and my God.

I also declare that because of the secret place and the shadow of Your powerful presence, You will deliver me from terror, arrows, pestilence and destruction.

God's Secret Place

Though I will see with my eyes and hear with my ears disturbing things, I walk by faith and not by sight.[iii] I will not be moved. Your Word is true and lives forever. "For Your Word is right and true and You are faithful in all You do (Psalm 33:4), and Your way is perfect" (Psalm 18:30).

Because of the declaration of my faith and my steadfast love towards You, You will promote me to the high place, be present with me and deliver me from all trouble, and grant me long life and eternity with You.

So Lord, for all these things, and more, I thank you and praise you.

In the matchless Name of Jesus, I pray.

Amen.

James 4:8.

John 15:7.

2 Corinthians 5:7.

Appendix Two

An Appeal

You have just read about **Psalm 91,** God's secret place, and an early warning for the future. The promises are real; they have been tested as fine steel, and they deliver to all without partiality.

Yet all of this could be entirely lost if one fails to receive the wonderful gift of the gospel. The gospel is the 'good news' of Jesus the Messiah, Son of God and Saviour. He took the penalty of our sin upon Himself by dying on the cross, and then rose again from the dead for our justification. This wonderful Bible word has two powerful meanings: first, justified people are declared 'not guilty;' second, justified people are declared 'righteous' before God.

How do we receive this great gospel of salvation, which is impossible to earn? We receive this indescribably wonderful gift by faith. Please consider:

God has a Plan: God's kingdom and your part in it have been known from before the foundation of the world (Ephesians 2:10).

You have A Problem: While everyone has issues and problems, this particular problem is the biggest and most deadly of all. It does not come from circumstances or the actions of others. This problem is called 'sin.' Sin means to 'miss the mark' or 'transgress God's holy standards.' Scripture is clear that everyone has a sin problem (Psalm 14:3; 53:3; Romans 3:10, 12, 23).

God's Secret Place

Sin has A High Price: Sin does not bring mere inconvenience or dissatisfaction. **Romans 6:23** is very clear that *"the wages of sin is death."* Left without remedy, our sin leaves us in a state of 'spiritual death,' then 'physical death', and eventually 'eternal death,' which means permanent separation from the source of all life, which is God.

There is Only One Remedy: Religion, good ideas, intentions, and works cannot take away sin. The only remedy is receiving God's free gift of redemption by believing the gospel. **Romans 10:9-10** says *"[t]hat if thou shalt confess with thy mouth the Lord Jesus, and shalt believe in thine heart that God hath raised him from the dead, thou shalt be saved. [10]For with the heart man believeth unto righteousness; and with the mouth confession is made unto salvation."*

The Application of the Remedy: It takes two things - repentance and faith, as affirmed by the Apostle Paul:

Testifying both to the Jews, and also to the Greeks, repentance toward God, and faith toward our Lord Jesus Christ (Acts 20:21).

Repentance: This means to 'change' our attitude and actions. It also means to 'turn.' Repentance implies that a person, heading in one direction, changes their mind, and turns in another direction. As Bible teacher Joy Dawson says, "Repentance means being sorry enough to quit." Without repentance, there is no salvation or revival.

Therefore leaving the principles of the doctrine of Christ, let us go on unto perfection; not laying again the foundation of repentance from dead works, and of faith toward God (Hebrews 6:1).

Faith: We receive Christ and the gospel by faith. Now is the day of salvation (2 Corinthians 6:2). Jesus stands at the door and knocks; if you will open the door, He will come in (Revelation 3:20). Open your heart

Appendix Two: An Appeal

wide and let the King of Glory come in (Psalm 24:7, 9). Receive Christ today by faith. Biblical faith means to:

- **Believe**: God says so, therefore, accept His Word at face value (Romans 10:9);

- **Receive**: Open your heart and let Him come in (John 1:12; Revelation 3:20);

- **Confess**: Faith is activated by confession. Confess Christ as Saviour and Lord (Romans 10:9);

Behold, I stand at the door, and knock: if any man hear my voice, and open the door, I will come in to him, and will sup with him, and he with me (Revelation 3:20).

- **Commit**: Surrender all to God. Commitment is the only way to obtain the full benefits of this great salvation (Psalm 37:5);

- **Trust**: Related to faith, trust is a solid confidence in God's ability, willingness, truthfulness, faithfulness, and reliability. We are called to trust God with all of our hearts, all of the time, even when on occasion, it does not make sense to the natural mind (Proverbs 3:5-6); God's ways and thoughts are higher and better than ours.

- **Obedience**: This is the bottom line, and without your obedience, every other aspect of faith fails. If Jesus is to be your Saviour and Lord, you must obey Him in all things, great or small. The renowned hymn said it so well: 'Trust and obey, for there's no other way to be happy in Jesus, than to trust and obey' (1 Samuel 15:22; Acts 5:29).

You may be a good, respectable person who believes in Jesus. You may attend church and even read the Bible. See, however, if you can answer the following questions:

- Have you ever asked Jesus Christ into your life (Romans 10:9-10; Revelation 3:20)?

- Is He living in your heart now (1 John 3:24)?

- Do you have 'peace with God' (Romans 5:1)?

- Do you know that your sins are forgiven and cleansed (1 John 1:9)?

- Do you have the 'new birth' (John 3:3)?

- Do you have the assurance of salvation (Romans 10:9-10)?

- Are you 'heaven-bound' (Hebrews 12:22-24)?

- Is your name written in the Lamb's Book of Life (Luke 10:20; Hebrews 12:23)?

If you cannot confidently say 'Yes' to all of these questions above, please say 'Yes' to this one:

> *Are you ready to receive Jesus Christ, here and now, as your personal Lord and Saviour? Are you prepared to make the wisest and most courageous decision of your life?*

If so, pray this simple prayer of repentance and faith, with sincerity and conviction, and you can then say 'Yes' to all.

A Prayer of Salvation

Heavenly Father, I am pleased to hear the gospel.
I acknowledge that Jesus is the Messiah, Son of God, and Saviour.
I confess that I am a sinner in need of salvation.

Appendix Two: An Appeal

I repent of all sins of the hands, head and heart.
As an act of my will, I say 'Yes' to the everlasting gospel, by inviting Jesus into my heart.
Come in, Lord Jesus, take full control, wash me from my sins in your shed blood, and deliver me from my sinful nature.
Thank you for the forgiveness of sins, the new birth, and the gift of eternal life.
By your grace, help me to live a God-honouring life,
In the Name of Your Son, My Saviour, Jesus Christ.

Amen.

Welcome to the family of God!

If you have prayed this prayer, please let us know. Our web address is tan.org.au or Teach All Nations, P.O. Box 493, Mount Waverley VIC 3149 Australia. Find a Bible-believing, Bible-based church and get involved in their discipleship program.

May your personal encounter with Jesus of Nazareth, Son of David, Son of God, Saviour bring you untold blessings in the days ahead. Let others know that you belong to Him. The first coming of Jesus changed the course of history; of that, there is no doubt. At His second coming, the world will not just be changed; it will be transformed.

Now that you have been born again, you will be able to appreciate **Psalm 91** and the entire Bible all the more and bask in the great blessings God is ready to bestow on you.

You are ready to dwell in the secret place.

Appendix Three

The Promises of Trusting God

Here is a more **extensive** list of promises God gives to those who trust in Him. The people who trust will receive:

1. **Protection**: they are protected and not forsaken (Psalm 9:10);

2. **A Fortress**: they are protected by God who is their rock, fortress, deliverer, strength, shield, and high tower (Psalm 18:2);

3. **The Shield of God**: they are safeguarded by God who becomes their defence (Psalm 18:30; Proverbs 30:5);

4. **No shame**: they are protected from shame (Psalm 25:2; 25:20; 31:1);

5. **Great Goodness**: they are beneficiaries of God's great goodness stored up for them (Psalm 31:19);

6. **Mercy**: they are witnesses to the wicked soaked in sorrow but they will be surrounded by mercy (Psalm 32:10);

7. **No Condemnation or Desolation**: they are protected from desolation and avoid condemnation (Psalm 34:22);

8. **Habitation in the land**: they will dwell in the land (of promise) and be fed (Psalm 37:3);

God's Secret Place

9. **God's Action**: God helps those who surrender their way to Him, and He brings things to pass (Psalm 37:5);

10. **Deliverance**: they are delivered by God who saves those who trust in Him (Psalm 37:40);

11. **Fearlessness**: they are not afraid of what man can do to them (Psalm 56:11);

12. **God as their Refuge**: they are sheltered by God who is their refuge (Psalm 62:8);

13. **Covering**: they are covered by God who is their refuge and fortress (Psalm 91:2);

14. **Shelter of God**: they are protected by God who will cover and shelter them (Psalm 91:4);

15. **God's Help and Shield**: they are protected by God who is their help and shield (Psalm 115:9);

16. **The Superiority of Trust in God**: they are blessed because they place their trust in God rather than put confidence in man (Psalm 118:8);

17. **Immovability**: they are immovable like Mount Zion and abide forever (Psalm 125:1);

18. **Divine Guidance**: they are blessed with divine direction (Proverbs 3:6);

19. **Prosperity**: they are enriched and prosperous (Proverbs 28:25);

20. **Safety**: they are safe because they forsake the fear of man, which is a snare; their trust in God will make them safe (Proverbs 29:25);

Appendix Three: The Promises of Trusting God

21. **Fearlessness**: they are not afraid because God is their strength, song, and salvation (Isaiah 12:2);

22. **Perfect Peace**: they are kept in perfect peace because their mind is on God (Isaiah 26:3);

23. **Everlasting strength**: they are recipients of God's everlasting strength (Isaiah 26:4);

24. **Light on their Path**: they are blessed with God's light on the path (Isaiah 50:10);

25. **Physical Protection**: they are delivered from danger and their life is spared (Jeremiah 39:18);

26. **God as their Sufficiency**: they are blessed with adequate provision from God; they will be 'God-sufficient,' not 'self-sufficient' (2 Corinthians 3:5).